F. Edward Westbrook

The two Hundredth Anniversary

Of the Erection of the Building Occupied as the Senate House of the State

of New York in 1777

F. Edward Westbrook

The two Hundredth Anniversary
Of the Erection of the Building Occupied as the Senate House of the State of New York in 1777

ISBN/EAN: 9783337154875

Printed in Europe, USA, Canada, Australia, Japan

Cover: Foto ©ninafisch / pixelio.de

More available books at **www.hansebooks.com**

The Two Hundredth Anniversary

OF THE ERECTION OF THE BUILDING

OCCUPIED AS THE SENATE HOUSE

Of the State of New York in 1777,

THE YEAR OF THE ADOPTION OF THE FIRST STATE CONSTITUTION, AT ESOPUS, (NOW CITY OF KINGSTON), TOGETHER WITH SKETCHES OF OLD PROMINENT CITIZENS OF KINGSTON, ETC., ETC.

Senate House of the State of New York. 1777. Nos. 5 and 7 Clinton Avenue. Kingston. N. Y.

Summer Residence of and belonging to FREDERICK E. WESTBROOK, Esq., of New York City.

Col. WESSEL TEN BROECK, born in Westphalia, 1635, erected this stone mansion about 1676, wherein the Senate of the State of New York was held in the year of the adoption of its first Constitution, 1777, and continued therein until the burning of Kingston by the British, October 16th, 1777.

BY FREDERICK EDWARD WESTBROOK,

Counsellor at Law and Member of the New York City Historical Society.

KINGSTON, N. Y. :
JOURNAL & FREEMAN BRANCH OFFICE PRINT, 43 WALL STREET.

1883.

HISTORICAL SKETCH.

In sketching the history of States, there are events which have occurred in prominent places of national importance which posterity loves to dwell upon and to commemorate. Remarkable deliverances from savage brutality and a painful record of their atrocities, as well as the calamities arising from Christian warfare, which are necessarily blended with the recollection of great distress or imminent peril, and whether as men or citizens we now greatly rejoice, by that very joy we expressly declare that our fathers once had cause to mourn.

Perpetual sunshine suits not the state of the natural world. Continued success is by no means favorable either to human happiness or virtue. The gloom incident to winter is the happiest recommendation of the return of the flowers of spring. The blessings of peace would be but imperfectly understood were it not for the antecedent anxieties resulting from the sorrows of war.

With reflections and feelings of this character relative to the great events incident to a retrospect of 200 years, particularly during the seventeenth century, that have occurred in this important place, successively known as Atkarkarton, Wiltwyck, Esopus, now the City of Kingston, N. Y., and which are immediately connected with the early Indian wars and with the wars of the American Revolution of 1776 and of 1812, which resulted with the permission and wisdom of the Supreme Ruler in the accomplishment of the independence of the United States, which is now the asylum of the oppressed of all lands who desire the advantages arising from a government humane and just in its moral sway over despotism, with its 50,000,000 inhabitants, will continue till the world eventually becomes educated, prepared and enabled to adopt a government similar in its character and in the enjoyment of like blessings.

The two hundredth anniversary of the erection of the walls of the venerable building now known as the Senate House of the State of New York, 1777, in the year of the adoption of its first constitution within its time-honored walls, which survived the ravages of fire and the power and efforts of the enemy in a desolating war, is a fitting and enduring monument to perpetuate the remembrance of those who fell in the service and contributed successfully in the accomplishment of the independence of their native or adopted land; the honest pride which arises within us on hearing what arduous struggles our ancestors endured to obtain such deliverances animates the heart to support and protect their memories.

We consider the earth as sacred where these heroes have long slept in death. This monumental building, its walls, if suffered to remain, will continue for centuries to come as a venerable relic of a heroic and suffering period; and the patriotic citizen as he passes by will exult in these vestiges of his country's glory, and feel an ardent hope (if necessary) that his name may hereafter be enrolled in the records of its fame. Our native land contains every enjoyment that this life can afford, and when existence terminates we all look to it for a grave where we can rest in peace; unassuming, vast in extent, powerful in resources, prompt in affording relief, firm and undismayed in danger, and merciful in victory, its 50,000,000 of inhabitants, separated from Europe by the stormy Atlantic, if united and relying upon that powerful Almighty arm that supported them in the infancy of their days, is capable on arriving at the manhood of their strength to humble any daring invader who may attempt to disturb the peaceful character of this nation, now the most powerful in the world. It displays mildness in its government and impartiality in its laws, which in this State is under a written constitution emanating from the people; its laws which govern and the hands which execute them are the creation of their wisdom and the representatives of their power.

In the luxuriance of youth and in the vigor of manhood it is wise to pause in our pursuits of business and pleasure, and to reflect upon the precious memories of the past. The barbarian Briton who defended his country at an early and rude period against the Roman invasion, driven to the remotest extremity of the land, rallied his followers to battle by the heart-stirring appeal: "Think of your fathers and your posterity." The lofty cliffs were covered with an army, whose firm resistance daunted the invaders, and though the Britons had only their naked limbs to oppose to the Roman armour, it required resolution and address even in veteran legions, before a fierce and bloody struggle terminated in gaining the shores. Continual storms destroyed or separated the fleet, which the perseverance of Cæsar renewed, and frequent sallies of British cavalry, and chariots from the woods and mountains checked the progress of devastation.

If in so imperfect a state of civilization the inhabitants of the British island could be thus attached to their caverns and forests, can there possibly exist the smallest doubt that their posterity in the new world will at all times act worthy of such distinguished ancestors!

One of the chief causes of the early prosperity of Rome is found in the cherished recollections of the virtues of its founders. No virtuous people will ever forget those by whom their infancy was cradled and defended. Those brave men who enlisted to support, sustain and protect the government of their country in the late civil strife, were animated and sustained in that great conflict by the powerful reflection that this was the government erected by their fathers which was shedding its benign influence over all lands, and was the only hope and consolation to the lovers of freedom and of civil and religious liberty.

At Esopus, now City of Kingston, N. Y., about the year 1676, Col. Wessel Ten Broeck erected the walls and finished the building since known as the Senate House of the State of New York, 1777. He was born in Westphalia, and was probably the great ancestor of all who bear his honored name in this State, being prominent in the church whose first clergyman was Rev. Mr. Blom, called in 1660; also was inducted into civil office about the year 1676 at Esopus, as the records of the Ulster County Clerk's office, N. Y., show in an affidavit made by him of that date that he was forty years of age, which was about the time of the erection of said building. Being a prominent man and in possession of what was then considered a large estate, he erected it in a substantial manner, which was considered at that early and rude period a large and grand building. The ceilings of Dutch houses generally are about six feet six inches. This house is eight feet seven inches in height, which now causes it still to become a pleasant building as a place of residence.

Col. Ten Broeck's family was composed of his wife, Jacomyntie, daughter of Rev. Laurentius Van Gaasbeek, and eight children, born at Esopus, now Kingston, between the years of 1670 and 1690. Their names are the following: John Ten Broeck; Jacob Ten Broeck; Mary Ten Broeck; Elsie Ten Broeck; Sarah Ten Broeck, who married Abraham Van Gaasbeek, who became owner of the Senate House through his wife, Sarah; Wessel Ten Broeck; Conrad Ten Broeck; Gertrude Ten Broeck, married John Dumont. John Dumont and Gertrude Ten Broeck (daughter of Col. Wessel Ten Broeck), his wife, had four children as follows: Rachel, who married Tjerck Beekman, who died in her 94th year, leaving an only child, Sarah Beekman, wife of the late Rev. Dr. Cornelius D. Westbrook; Gertrude, who died unmarried; Sarah Dumont, who married Hon. Peter Van Gaasbeek; Mary Dumont, married John Ten Broeck; John Dumont, married Sarah and Elizabeth Waring. He died in 1869, in his 95th year.

Abraham Van Gaasbeek, who married Sarah, daughter of Col. Wessel Ten Broeck as aforesaid, was the uncle of Sarah Dumont. He devised the building known as the Senate House and his personal estate by will (see book C, page 72, in County Clerk's office, Kingston, Ulster County) to his loving niece Sarah Dumont, who afterwards became the wife of Hon. Peter Van Gaasbeek, only son of said Abraham Van Gaasbeek. Said Hon. Peter Van Gaasbeek and Sarah Dumont his wife had an only child surviving, Sarah Van Gaasbeek, who became owner of said Senate House on the death of her mother as sole heir at law. On the death of Sarah Van Gaasbeek, about 1850, by her last will and testament she devised the Senate House and grounds and other property to her cousin, Charles Ruggles Westbrook, son of the late Rev. Dr. Cornelius D. Westbrook. In April, 1869, Charles R. Westbrook and wife conveyed by deed the Senate House and grounds to his brother, Frederick E. Westbrook, of the city of New York, the present owner. From the above record of title the building and grounds have been in possession of Col. Wessel Ten Broeck and his heirs from 1676 to the year 1869.

We will now return to Col. Wessel Ten Broeck, who married as his second wife the widow of Thomas Chambers, the first prominent settler of Wiltwyck or Esopus, now Kingston, and late owner of the manor of Foxhall, 1698. Her only son, Abraham Van Gaasbeek, by a former husband, Rev. Laurentius Van Gaasbeek, second minister of the Reformed Dutch Church of Wiltwyck or Esopus, now Kingston, from 1667 to 1680, on his death became owner of the manor of Foxhall, devised by his stepfather, Thomas Chambers (her second husband), on condition of his assuming the name of Abraham Van Gaasbeek Chambers. The descendants of Col. Wessel Ten Broeck and Van Gaasbeek have owned and occupied this Senate House of 1777 for near two centuries.

In the records of the Ulster County Historical Society in the year 1860 in book part 2, page 124, is the following : " The Senate (of 1777) sat at the house of Abraham Van Gaasbeek, a stone building constructed after the then Esopus fashion, the last one on the west side of East Front street, now known as Clinton avenue, near the junction of that street with North Front street. This fact was shown by an entry on the journal of the Provincial Convention, its own records, not mentioning any room. This house has recently been occupied by Rev. Dr. Cornelius D. Westbrook." The late Mrs. Mary Ten Broeck, the grand-daughter of Col. Wessel Ten Broeck, and wife of the late John Ten Broeck, of Flatbush, near Kingston, who died about thirty years ago, over ninety years of age, confirms what has been said relating to the time of the erection of this building in a conversation with the writer before her death. She had a family record to the present time.

There have been many articles written which have been published. I will select one of them, written by a well-known writer, Miss Margaret Winslow, of Brooklyn, N. Y.

[From the New York Observer.]

THE BUILDING ERECTED IN 1676.

THE OLDEST PUBLIC BUILDING IN THE UNITED STATES—ONCE A SENATE CHAMBER—THE GREAT MEN IT HAS SHELTERED—OTHER HISTORIC STRUCTURES.

"Ulster County is rich in material of historic interest. Many of these are associated with this venerable house in which we are now sheltered. It is a quaint mansion, you may be sure, with solid stone walls nearly two feet in thickness in front, while the back is built of scarcely discolored brick brought from Holland at least two centuries ago: for the house was built in 1676 by the ancestor of our host, one Colonel Wessel Ten Broeck, who was born in Westphalia in 1635, elected a *schoppen* or public officer in 1670, and then appointed to superintend the settlement of the *nieuw dorp*, or the villages of Hurley and Marbletown. The Colonel intermarried with the Van Gaasbeck family, had eight children, and from the descendant of one of these—Sarah Van Gaasbeck, great-grand-daughter of the Patroon, Thomas Chambers, *alias* Clabbort—it came, by will, into the possession of the present owner, Frederick E. Westbrook, Esq., a New York lawyer. The well-known Dutch pride of ancestry is in this case quite overshadowed by the pride of its owner in the possession of 'the oldest *public* building in the United States.' In 1869 he commenced repairing the old house, which was in its day considered one of remarkable grandeur, its length being seventy feet and height eight feet seven inches—the usual Dutch measurement of the period being only six feet. The original beams of prepared oak in the cellar and ceiling were found in perfect condition, also the sloping garret with its five bed-rooms. The *linto* (lean-to) kitchen, only six feet high, was also perfect, but the roofs have been added since the Revolution, such light woodwork having all perished in the conflagration of the town in 1777. The antiquary has altered the interior as little as possible, to make it habitable, and has gathered in the seven old rooms, which all lay side by side, a heterogeneous mass of old furniture, paintings, engravings and historical records; while above one of the many outside doors he has placed the inscription:

Colonel Wessel Ten Broeck erected this house in 1676, wherein the Senate of New York was held during the adoption of its first Constitution, 1777.

An evening spent in such an atmosphere of antiquity cannot but be interesting, and the hours fled rapidly by as we conversed of the stirring events which the old house had seen and the great men it had sheltered. Here Ten Broeck, Pierre Van Cortlandt, Gansevoort, Governor Morris, Robert R. Livingston, Colonel DeWitt, Samuel Townsend, General Scott, Colonel Broome and others carried on their deliberations concerning the form of government to be adopted by the new State, and in one of these low-roofed chambers, in all probability, John Jay drew the draft of the Constitution which was adopted at the 'Constitution House'—the old Bogardus Inn, which till quite recently stood on the corner of Maiden Lane and Fair street, and in which the first 'Assembly' of the State of New York met—with but one dissenting voice, preparatory to its promulgation from a platform erected on a barrel head April 22, 1777.

Here from time to time have come the great men whom Kingston has either received or sent forth into public life. Here Gen. Armstrong, the boy hero of the Revolution, father-in-law of William B. Astor and ex-Secretary of War, lived in 1804, previous to his departure as Minister to the French Court, leaving a small marble fireplace, the first ever seen in Kingston, as a memorial of his residence ; and here, last spring, Gen. Arthur, the Republican candidate for Vice-President, bowed his tall head to escape collision with the time-honored and smoke-begrimed rafters ; and here we —the honored Drs. Van Santvoord and Hoes, with the host and the writer —sat and discussed the history of Kingston : its first and second Indian wars, 1659 and 1661, and the burning of the fort, 1663 ; Stuyvesant's treaty of peace, 1661, at which period the wily savages ceded him the land on which the city now stands, ' to grease his feet' in return for the compliment of his visit, on which occasion the renowned warrior changed the Dutch name of Esopus, or Groote Esopus, variously stated to be derived from the Latin fabulist and from a soft place, to Wiltwyck, or Wild man's village. The Dutch regained the town after its capture along with the Swedish possessions east of the Hudson in 1664, holding it, however, only for a very short time, as said one of my informants, adding thereto much of the intermediate history till its consolidation with Rondout and Wilbur into a city in 1872, and the building of the splendid new City Hall and Armory, the latter only just completed.

There are many other buildings and several localities of special interest to those who love the mild antiquities of our brand-new country—the Academy founded in 1774, in which DeWitt Clinton and Thomas DeWitt, Edward Livingston, Stephen Van Rensselaer and Abram Van Vechten received their early education ; the stone Court House built in 1818 upon the site of a much older one ; and the First Dutch Church, organized August, 1659, by Rev. Hermanus Blom, sent from Holland as a candidate, and ordained by the Classis of Amsterdam, 1660. The fac-similes of signatures of the fifteen successors of Blom, carefully gathered by the venerable Dr. Hoes, and shown me at the close of our pleasant evening conversation, are sufficient guarantee that, from the first, Esopus—Wiltwyck—Kingston has been in the care of that blessed people ' whose God is the Lord.' "

The following letter was sent to the President of the New York Historical society, which was published by the Kingston *Journal*, and also in the History of Ulster County. The following copy thereof was published in the Fishkill *Standard :*

THE KINGSTON "SENATE HOUSE."

The following letter was read at the stated meeting of the New York Historical Society, on the first Tuesday of May, 1878, before a learned and appreciative audience of ladies and gentlemen. The " Senate House" was the centre of attraction at the Kingston Centennial last year. It is owned and occupied by Mr. Frederick E. Westbrook, who is a son of the late Rev. Dr. Cornelius D. Westbrook, for twenty-five years pastor of the Reformed Dutch Church, Fishkill Village, and held in affectionate remembrance by many of the older citizens of this town :

9

NEW YORK, May 3, 1878.

HON. FRED. DePEYSTER, LL. D., PRESIDENT OF THE NEW YORK HISTO-
RICAL SOCIETY :

RESPECTED AND DEAR SIR :—At the State Centennial held at Kingston, N. Y., July 30, 1877, the old house owned by myself and known as
" the Senate House" in the year of its adoption of the first Constitution of
this State, April, 1777, wherein great interest was manifested by the large
numbers who thronged its spacious rooms on that memorable occasion, the
small marble fireplace erected by General Armstrong, father-in-law of the
late William B. Astor, Esq., and ex-Secretary of War, who occupied this
house as his place of residence in 1804 and until his departure as Minister
to the French Court as successor to his brother-in-law, Chancellor Livingston, was particularly noticed. Your records and proceedings of the Ulster Historical Society recognize this house as the place where the Senate
of 1777 held its sessions.

Colonel Wessel Ten Broeck, born in Westphalia in 1635, erected this
house about the year 1676, was the head of all that bear his honored name
in this State, intermarried with the Van Gaasbeck family, whose joint descendants are prominent and numerous. Rev. Laurentius Van Gaasbeek,
second minister of the Reformed Dutch Church of Wiltwyck, now City of
Kingston, from 1667 to 1680, on his death, Colonel Thomas Chambers,
then owner of the manor of Foxhall, the first prominent settler of. Wiltwyck or Esopus, now Kingston, married his widow : and on the death of
Chambers in 1698, Colonel Wessel Ten Broeck (aforesaid) married the
widow of Chambers, all prominent in the records of Kingston. Rev. Blom,
the first minister, settled here in 1660. Chambers, Ten Broeck and Swartwout the scout were prominent in driving out the savages during the Indian massacre of 1663 and the wars which succeeded, in which the illustrious Petrus Stuyvesant himself took a prominent part.

With these brief reasons, together with the interest so recently manifested in hearing the paper read (at last meeting, before a learned, polished
and large audience), respecting old houses in Kinderhook, induces me to
offer the society, of which you are its honored head, a photograph, framed,
of this " old Senate House, 1777." I gave a copy thereof to the authorities of the City of Kingston, and the other I respectfully offer for your acceptance. I remain, dear sir, your friend and obedient servant,

FREDERICK E. WESTBROOK.

A sketch of this building was published in the *Magazine of History*, ed-
ited by John A. Stevens, late librarian of the New York Historical Society. A photograph copy thereof is in the work entitled " The Centennial
Celebrations of the State of New York," published by direction of the Legislature of the State of New York, under the direction of the Secretary of
State, at the time of the Centennial, July 30, 1877. There was a splendid
military procession together with an elegant display of fireworks. This day
was the one hundredth anniversary of the inauguration of the State government.

The following article, with illustrations of the Senate House of 1777 appeared in *Harper's Weekly*, August, 1877 :

NEW YORK'S CENTENNIAL.

The old and picturesque town of Kingston presented a lively appearance on Monday, July 30, when the hundredth anniversary of the inauguration of the first Governor of the State of New York and the formation of the State government was celebrated. Kingston is peculiarly constructed. " The historic portion, or old Kingston," says the correspondent of the New York *World*, "occupies a level plain nearly two miles from the centre of the lower portion, which is Rondout. In the upper portion can be found the same old houses that the British essayed to burn, at least forty-eight of them, which present nearly the same appearance as they did one hundred years ago, when General Vaughn's troops burned the burgh. A peculiarity has been noticed regarding these old houses—that those of great pretensions and considerable dimensions were almost totally destroyed, or burned so as to require the relaying of considerable portions of their walls. But the smaller houses remained intact, and only required refitting as to their inside wood-work, which was of insignificant proportions, and only enough of it to really improve by its burning the blue limestone of which the houses were constructed. So there are now four dozen old stone houses, with thick walls and low roofs, which were baptized by fire and yet remain." The house in which the New York State Senate met during the year 1777 is still standing. It is the property of Mr. Frederick E. Westbrook, a prominent citizen of Ulster County.

Our illustrations on page 648 show various phases of the celebration. The weather was propitious, heavy showers in the morning having laid the dust, and light clouds mitigating the heat of the midsummer sun. At noon a large procession was formed, composed of military organizations, civic societies, trades, firemen, and official bodies. It made a line over a mile long, and numbered more than five thousand persons. The procession was reviewed by the Mayor and Common Council of the city, and paraded through the principal streets, passing the interesting historic spots of the place, including the old house where the first State Senate met, the house where the Constitution was adopted, and the Court House where Governor George Clinton was inaugurated one hundred years ago.

The procession then marched to the grounds where the celebration was held. The Mayor of Kingston presided. The ceremonies were opened by prayer by the Rev. J. G. Van Slyke, pastor of the First Reformed Dutch Church, organized in 1659. Judge Westbrook then delivered an address of welcome, on the conclusion of which the Rev. Dr. J. C. F. Hoes, a venerable ex-pastor of the First Reformed Church, read a letter from Rev. Dr. Doll, pastor of that church, to Governor Clinton, prefacing it with the remark that General Vaughan at first hesitated about destroying the church, " but after learning the prominent part its pastor, consistory and membership had taken in patriotic enterprises, he hesitated no longer, but applied the torch to the house of God." In this letter, which is dated August 2, 1777, Rev. Mr. Doll congratulates the Governor upon his being raised to distinguished power, and says, " All ranks, in placing you at their head, have pledged their lives and fortunes to support and defend you in this exalted station, and the consistory of Kingston cheerfully unite in the implicit stipulation, and promise you their prayers."

The orator of the day, the Hon. Chauncey M. Depew, was then introduced. In a very interesting address he sketched the history of the State from its formation to the present day.

The Court House standing in 1777 at Kingston, together with the building where the first Constitution was adopted, having been taken down, and this Senate House of 1777 being the only building now standing of a public character to commemmorate events of the Revolution, causes this ancient building, together with Washington's Headquarters at Newburgh, to become by far the most important public buildings as relics now standing in this State.

Holland, in the 17th century, was the most prosperous commercial state in Europe, the principal corporation the Dutch East India Company : under its auspices the Hudson River was discovered and explored in 1609 as far as what is now known as Albany, N. Y.; their flag was hoisted on Manhattan Island in 1613; a few huts were erected for the purpose of trading with the Indians. A few traders as early as 1614 found their way to what was afterwards known as Fort Orange (now Albany) and at Wiltwyck (now Kingston). A few years subsequent Fort Orange (now Albany) was built, and a fort at the mouth of the Rondout, Atkarkarton (now Kingston).

In 1621 the Dutch West India Company was formed, with the exclusive right to trade on both coasts of America. The province of New Netherlands fell under the control of this corporation and its actual settlement was commenced.

In 1624 Peter Minneck was sent out from Amsterdam as Governor of the Colony, and brought over with him some French colonists, who were in reality the first settled inhabitants of New Netherlands ; the few emigrants or traders with the Indians who preceded them were not entitled to the name of settlers. Shortly afterwards the Indian title to Manhattan Island was purchased by Kieft for about $24. A block house was erected at its southern extremity which was called Fort Amsterdam.

In 1629 a more extensive colonization was organized in Holland and ratified by the States General, conditioned that any member of the company who would emigrate fifty persons upwards of fifteen years should become absolute possessor of a colony sixteen miles in extent along the shore or navigable river. He was to reign like a Feudel Lord under the title of Patroon, but the settlers were allowed as much land as they could cultivate and freedom from taxation for ten years. It was stipulated that the lands should be first purchased from the Indians, as the lawful and original owners of the land.

Thomas Chambers brought a small number of families in 1652 and began the actual settlement of Ulster County. Rev. Mr. Miller was sent to New Amsterdam as a Missionary by the Episcopal Church of England ; as they had no church building he occasionally preached in the Dutch Church erected in the fort at New Amsterdam in 1642.

On his return he published in London, in 1695, Miller's History of New York, in which were plans of three places of strength, New Amsterdam (now New York), Fort Orange (now Albany), and at Esopus (now Kingston). They continued to be the three most important places till the year Kingston was burned, 1777.. Kingston was laid out, and the title was obtained from the savages and presented to Stuyvesant. Constant difficulties and loss of life occurred with the ravages until after the massacre of Wiltwyck in 1663. Dominie Blom, the first minister settled in 1660, has related the facts relative to this awful event. A charter was obtained May 16, 1661, municipal power granted to Wiltwyck, Pell, Sleight and Roosa were appointed *schepens*, and Roeliff Swartwout, Sheriff. Captain Thomas Chambers, Justice at Esopus, for signal services in the time of the Indian war, his house was erected into Manor of Foxhall. This Manor House was, without doubt, at what is now known as Rondout, on the site of Mr. Jansen Hasbrouck's grounds : being a prominent man and of great wealth for that period, he might subsequently had his residence elsewhere. With all his temporal honors, having no children, his second wife was the widow of Rev. Laurentius Van Gaasbeck, whose son assumed the name of Abraham Van Gaasbeck Chambers, who became sole heir to the Manor of Foxhall on the death of his step-father, Thomas Chambers, in 1696. The widow of Chambers thereupon married the said Col. Wessel TenBroeck, the then owner of the building now known as the Senate House of the State of New York, 1777.

William Beekman, the great-ancester of those who bear his name, was Sheriff of Kingston until the close of Governor Lovelace's administration in 1674, when he returned to New York. He was born in Germany, emigrated to America : after filling many official positions and in possession of great wealth he died in 1707 with distinguished reputation. The present William and Beekman streets, New York, bear his name. Henry, his eldest son, settled at Kingston, was Judge of Ulster County and member of the Provincial Legislature. His daughter Margaret married Robert R. Livingston, and among her children was Jane, wife of General Montgomery, who fell at the seige of Quebec. Chancellor Robert R. Livingston and his sister, who married General John Armstrong, U. S. Senator, Secretary of War, &c., occupied the building now known as the Senate House in 1802 and until he left as Minister to France.

The English Conquest commenced in 1664 ; Nichols assumed the government as Deputy Governor under the Duke of York of all his territories in America.

New Amsterdam was now called New York in honor of the Duke of York, and Fort Orange, Albany. At this time the Dutch inhabitants in the colony numbered about 6,000. New Amsterdam contained 3,000, nearly one-half of that number. After the conquest by the English many returned to Holland.

Their habitations, however, were soon occupied by emigrants partly from Great Britain, but mostly from New England. Upon the Hudson River were many Dutch settlers who remained.

Colonel Lovelace succeeded Nichols in the government of the colony.

Kingston, formerly known as Atkarkarton, Wiltwyck and Esopus, had a few settlers who located among the Esopus Indians in 1614.

Rev. J. Megapolensis, third minister of the Collegiate Dutch Church of New York, in a letter on the state of religion in the province of New York, to the classes of Amsterdam, dated August 5, 1657, says : " Thomas Chambers and a few others removed to Atkarkarton, or Esopus (now Kingston), an exceedingly beautiful land, in 1652, and began the actual settlement of Ulster county ; it was also known among the savages as the Pleasant Land."

From the date of the first settling of this place, the following are the names of the Director-Generals of the Province of New York, sent out from Holland : Andrisen Jores, whose administration commenced in 1623 ; Cornelius Jacobsen May, William Verhulst, Peter Minuit, under whose administration, in 1626, Manhattan Island (New York) was purchased from the Indians for $24. Then follow Wouter Van Twiller, William Kieft, and last the valiant, energetic, able and faithful Petrus Stuyvesant, whose administration commenced May 11, 1647, in whom the early settlers of Kingston, long harrassed by the savages, found a powerful friend.

The wars with the Indians and negotiations and troubles with his English neighbors continued till New Amsterdam surrendered to the English in 1664, when Stuyvesant (released from the vexations and turmoils of public life), after visiting Holland, returned to New York and spent the rest of his days in retirement on his " Bowerie," where he departed his useful life in 1671.

General military officers for the colonies appointed by Congress June, 1775 :

George Washington, Commander-in-Chief; Artemus Ward, Charles Lee, Philip Schuyler and Israel Putnam were appointed Major-Generals ; Seth Pomeroy, Richard Montgomery, David Wooster, William Heath, Joseph Spencer, John Thomas, John Sullivan and Nathaniel Green were appointed Brigadier-Generals, and Horatio Gates, Adjutant-General.

The revolutionary authority in New York was exercised by a Provincial Convention assembled in the Exchange, New York city, April 20, 1775.

Charles DeWitt, George Clinton and Levi Paulding were delegates from Ulster County.

Members from this county in the subsequent First Provincial Congress, which met at New York May 23, 1775, were Colonel Charles Hardenbergh, of Rosendale, Colonel James Clinton, Egbert Dumont, of Kingston, Charles Clinton, Christopher Tappen, of Kingston, John Nicholson and Jacob Hornbeck, of Rochester.

Second Provincial Congress met at New York November 14, 1775. Members from this county were Henry Wisner, Jr., Matthew Rea, Dirck Wynkoop, Jr., Matthew Cantine, Andries DeWitt, Andries Lefevre, Thomas Palmer and Samuel Brewster.

Third Provincial Congress met at New York May 14, 1776. Members from Ulster were Colonel Charles DeWitt, Colonel Abraham Hasbrouck, Colonel James Snyder, Matthew Cantine, Matthew Rea, Arthur Park, Henry Wisner, Jr., and Samuel Brewster.

Fourth Provincial Congress assembled at White Plains, in Westchester County, July 9, 1776, when the Declaration of Independence was immediately adopted, and on the following day the name of the house was changed to that of the " Convention of the Representatives of the State of New York." Members from Ulster were Matthew Cantine, Colonel Charles DeWitt, Major Arthur Parks, Colonel Levi Paulding, Matthew Rea, Christopher Tappen, Colonel Johannes Hardenbergh and Henry Wisner, Jr.

Convention adjourned to Fishkill August 29, 1776. From there it moved to Kingston, Ulster County, N. Y., where a committee was appointed, of which John Jay was chairman, to report the draft of a Constitution. After discussion the report of the committee was accepted, and the first Constitution of the State of New York was adopted on the 20th of April, 1777, and was proclaimed at the Court House at Kingston at 11 o'clock A. M. on the 22d of April, 1777, and on the 13th of May, 1777, the convention adjourned, leaving power in the hands of a Council of Safety.

The first election under the constitution was held July 30, 1777. George Clinton was declared Governor of the State of New York in the presence of the military and citizens assembled at Kingston.

Among other important events of the eventful year 1777 was the sacking and burning of Kingston by the British forces under General Vaughan, known in history as Vaughan's second expedition. A paper prepared by Hon. George W. Pratt was read before the Ulster Historical Society relative to the event on the 16th of October, 1860, being the 83d anniversary of its burning. This eminent man fell early in life, in public service (in the late war), universally lamented and respected, and if his life had been spared this important society would still be in operation, in accordance with the wish (as expressed to the writer) of its late honored president, Abraham

Bruyn Hasbrouck. It is to be hoped that his desire will be complied with and this important society soon reorganized and continue its valuable services.

The writer will sketch a few of the prominent men of Ulster County in the service under the Colonial and State Governments, distinguished in the annals of Ulster County :

Robert R. Livingston was appointed Chancellor of the State : John Jay, Chief Justice, and Robert Gales and John Sloss Hobert, Associate Justices of the Supreme Court ; John Mann, Secretary of State ; Egbert Benson, Attorney-General, and Comfort Sands, Adjutant-General.

Governor Clinton married Cornelia Tappen, sister of Christopher Tappen, of Kingston. He was born July 26, 1739, and departed this life full of years and full of honors, at Washington City, on the 20th of April, 1812.

John Jay was born in the city of New York December 12, 1745 ; married Sarah, daughter of William Livingston : he was the alleged author of the first constitution of the State of New York, appointed under it Chief Justice of the Supreme Court of the State of New York. The first term thereof was held at Kingston, N. Y., September 9th, 1777. He was afterwards appointed by President Washington Chief Justice of the Supreme Court of the United States, and subsequently elected Governor of the State of New York. This learned and accomplished man (of Huguenot descent) died at Bedford May 17, 1829. He left the example of a well spent life, an unspotted name, and his illustrious services will always hold an important place in the history of his native State.

Col. Johannes Hardenbergh, son of the patentee of the Hardenbergh Patent, was a member of the Colonial Assembly from 1737 to 1743, and of the State Legislature in 1781-2. Departed this life August 29, 1786, aged 80 years ; a true friend of church and State. When General Washington visited Ulster county, June, 1783, Colonel Hardenbergh entertained Mrs. Washington, with Governor and Mrs. Clinton, at his house in Rosendale.

Egbert Dumont, Sheriff of Ulster county under George III. of England, from 1771 to 1773 ; from the first he espoused the cause of the Revolution, and was a deputy in the Provincial Congress which met in May, 1775. He was again Sheriff from 1775 to 1781, and from 1788 to 1789. Prominent in public affairs.

Col. Levi Paulding, of Marbletown, appointed Colonel of the Ulster County Militia from October 25, 1775, to July, 1776. Subsequently delegate to the Provincial Convention, 1775 ; also of Congresses of 1776 and 1777. Appointed first Judge of the county of Ulster May, 1777, and held the office till his death, in 1782.

Cornelius C. Schoonmaker, of Shawangunk, was Member of Assembly nearly seven years, from 1777 to 1795; from 1791 to 1793 Member of Congress: was a delegate to the Constitutional Convention of 1778. He died in 1796. Hon. Marius Schoonmaker was his grandson.

Jacob Hornbeck, of Rochester, appointed Lieutenant-Colonel of Paulding's regiment, chairman of the Rochester Committee of Safety, and in 1775 a deputy of the first Provincial Congress. Died 1778, and buried at Rochester, Ulster county.

Captain Tjerck Beckman was an officer of the Revolution and an original member of the Society of Cincinnati. Died at Kingston December 25, 1791. He was father of the late Sarah, wife of Rev. Dr. C. D. Westbrook, deceased, died about the year 1793. His grand son John Westbrook is the present member of the Society of Cincinnati.

Colonel Abraham Hasbrouck, son of Joseph, and grandson of Abraham. Hasbrouck, one of the twelve proprietors of the New Paltz Patent, was born in 1707 near New Paltz; in 1735 he removed to Kingston. On the 5th of January, 1738, he married Catharine, daughter of Jacobus Bruyn, of Shawangunk. In 1737 was Colonel of Ulster County Militia; member of the Colonial Assembly, 1739 to 1745, and from 1759 to 1768. After a life of prominence in his country's service, he departed this life November 16, 1791, and was buried with military honors at Kingston.

A younger brother, Colonel Jonathan Hasbrouck, of this period, resided in the house commonly called Washington's Headquarters, at Newburgh. He was born about the year 1722; married Tryntje (Catharine), daughter of Cornelius BuBois, and shortly after removed to Newburgh, where he continued till his death, July 31, 1780. Col. Hasbrouck enlarged the house at Newburgh well-known as "Washington's Headquarters," and it remained in the possession of the family nearly a century, till it became the property of the State and cared for by the Trustees of the village of Newburgh.

After Governor Clinton the most prominent man in Ulster county was Charles DeWitt, of Greenkill. Before the Colonies separated from Great Britain he represented the county in the Colonial Assembly from 1768 to 1775; resolute and patriotic; was a member of the Provincial Assembly in 1775, and subsequent Congresses, and also on the Committee of Safety, appointed Colonel in 1775. He was a member of the convention appointed to draft a Constitution adopted 1777. In 1784 he was chosen a delegate to Congress. From 1781 to 1785 he was a Member of Assembly, till his death, April 27, 1787.

General Frederick Westbrook was an officer of the Revolution of 1776, and a Brigadier-General in the war of 1812. Born at Rochester, Ulster county, N. Y.; he married Sarah Depew. He was a true patriot in the cause of his country, and departed this life after a lingering illness at the residence of his son, Rev. Dr. C. D. Westbrook, at Fishkill, N. Y., 1823, in the 74th year of his age.

Rev. Dr. Cornelius D. Westbrook was the last of the eminent men who lived in and departed this life in the Senate House of 1777, and therefore a brief notice of him will be given. He was born at Rochester, Ulster county, N. Y., May 8, 1782, and was the only child of General Frederick Westbrook and Sarah Depew his wife. Gen. Westbrook was an officer of the Revolution of 1776 and of the war of 1812, of Anglo-Saxon and Huguenot ancestry. An extended history of Dr. Westbrook's life appears in Rev. Dr. Corwin's History of the Dutch Church, and in the History of Ulster county : also an interesting sketch of his life from the pen of Rev. Dr. C. Van Santvoord, of Kingston. Dr. Westbrook departed this life at Kingston, N. Y., March, 1858. Many resolutions were passed relative to his life and services, of which the following only will be inserted :

At a meeting of the South Classis of New York City, held April 20, 1858, it was

Resolved, That the stated clerk be requested to forward to the family of the late Rev. Dr. Westbrook the following tribute to his memory :

" After a long, active and useful life, Rev. Cornelius D. Westbrook, D.
" D., for many years a member of this Classis, a Father in Israel and a
" veteran in the camp of Christ, has been gathered to his Fathers in peace
" and in honour : in him all the best purposes in the life of man have been
" accomplished, and he came to the grave in full age, like as a shock of
" corn cometh in his season."

The only members which composed the Rev. Dr. Westbrook's family who resided at his late residence at the Senate House were his widow Sarah Beekman, and her devoted daughter Mary, afterwards the wife of James L. Van Deusen, Esq.

Severyn Bruyn was born at Esopus (now Kingston) May 25, 1726, and departed this life at Kingston, August 19, 1759. He married Catharine TenBroeck, grand-daughter of Col. Wessel TenBroeck. He was an eminent citizen.

Lieutenant-Colonel Jacobus Severyn Bruyn, his son, was born at Kingston, N. Y., October 27, 1751. He served as an officer in our Revolutionary struggle and was an original member of the Society of Cincinnati. He married Miss Blandina Elmendorf, of Kingston, who was eminent for her intellectual attainments. Two sons were their only descendants, Edward and Severyn. Col. Bruyn departed this life at Kingston July 12, 1825. He was distinguished as an officer and for his great services during the war : he afterwards served with distinction in the councils of the State.

Severyn Bruyn, his son, married Catharine Hasbrouck, daughter of Judge Jonathan Hasbrouck. He was a gentleman by nature and education, be-

2

loved in every circle which he honored. After a few years spent in the practice of the law he accepted the position of cashier of a bank ; when his services were ended he retired from business. He was a true patriot, a scholar, and a Christian gentleman. He departed this life in peace, and left the presence of his family and friends, by whom he was greatly beloved, and with the affectionate regrets of the entire community where he resided, October 27. 1856, leaving two children, Augustus Hasbrouck Bruyn, Esq., and the late Mrs. Mary Bruyn Forsyth.

Hon. Abraham Bruyn Hasbrouck, LL. D., a prominent lawyer of Kingston, son of Judge Jonathan Hasbrouck, was Member of Congress, and for ten years President of Rutger's College. He was the recipient of honors, bestowed by the synod of the oldest church in the State, the Reformed Dutch Church in America, assembled at Kingston a few years ago. At an appointed hour, by previous arrangement, this learned body received Mr. Hasbrouck, standing : a speech was delivered by its President on this occasion, which was replied to by Mr. Hasbrouck in a learned and dignified address befitting so important an occasion. No greater honor could be bestowed. He departed this life in peace and in honor at Kingston, N. Y., February 23, 1879.

Hon. Lucas Elmendorf, one of Kingston's most honored sons, was possessed of a brilliant intellect, well read in the law and in the routine of its practice, especially relating to titles of real estate in Ulster county, which fifty years ago enlisted and occupied the attention of the most eminent minds in the State : his learning and counsel in their investigations was of great service. The writer believes too little has been said of this great man. As a statesman, his broad and liberal views at this period were felt and acknowledged in the National and State councils. His influence, without doubt, contributed largely to the appointment of Professor Henry to be the head of Smithsonian Institute at Washington. I have before me copy of a letter written by Professor Henry, dated September 22, 1876, in answer to an application made by the Hon Wm. Coventry H. Waddell in behalf of Misses Julia and Nellie, daughters of the late Nicholas Elmendorf, of Kingston, for a photograph of the Professor, who was the distinguished friend of their grandfather, Hon. Lucas Elmendorf, and was associated with him in the survey, &c., of the old Lucas Turnpike road. Professor Henry, in his reply, sending his photograph, says : " I should take special interest in visiting again the mansion of your grand old relative, Judge Lucas Elmendorf. His stately form and expressive countenance is now before me, and I have never recalled him to recollection but with feelings of gratitude, admiration and respect. We formed on a short acquaintance a warm friendship, which continued during life. He did me the favor, unsolicited, to exert an influence in my advancement in life." This is the language of that great man,

Professor Henry, of Smithsonian Institute. The offices held by Judge Lucas Elmendorf are as follows: He was Member of Congress from 1797 to 1803 ; Member of Assembly, 1804 ; District Attorney from 1801 to 1811 : Regent of the University from 1805 to 1829 : State Senator from 1816 to 1817 : County Judge from 1818 to 1821 ; Surrogate of Ulster County from 1835 to 1840. He departed this life in the year 1843 at Albany, with the regrets of his family, the community, and the State to which he contributed his eminent services for their welfare and happiness.

Hon. Charles H. Ruggles was Vice-Chancellor Circuit Judge of the Supreme Court of the State of New York, appointed in 1831. He was elected Judge of the Court of Appeals in 1847. He was an uncle of Hon. Theodoric R. Westbrook, Judge of the Supreme Court of New York. His character was exalted as a man and as a jurist. He died with distinguished reputation about the year 1875.

Jacob Burhans, son of Cornelius and Maria (TenBroeck) Burhans, was born August 30, 1792. In the year 1816 he became a clerk for his uncle, Jacob TenBroeck (a descendant of Col. Wessel TenBroeck, the elder), and subsequently was clerk to Judge Jonathan Hasbrouck. He commenced business as a merchant for himself in 1820 and continued till 1846, when ill health caused him to retire from active duties as a merchant. He contributed to organize four banks in Kingston, and was the first President of the State of New York Bank ; was a prominent member and officer of the First Reformed Dutch Church of Kingston ; was for many years a trustee of the Kingston Academy, and was deeply interested in the cause of education. The delineations of the countenance of this good man inspired respect. The writer in his youthful days saw him frequently in the church he so faithfully served and was fascinated with his dignified, mild and placid countenance, indicative of the man, and left an impression on his boyish mind that the lapse of time has never been able to efface from his memory. He had eight children, two of whom, Cornelius and John Salisbury Burhans, are well-known merchants, and one of his daughters married Hon. Frederick L. Westbrook, all of this city. This true Christian left the presence of his numerous relatives with their painful regrets, and this community joined with them in sorrow for their loss and respect for his precious memory. He departed in peace and in honor, and rested in cheerful anticipation of a happy immortal life. He has left his friends the example of such a life and the glory of such a death.

A brief sketch of the noble race of men will now be given who so powerfully contributed in the stormy period of our Revolutionary struggle, who have long since passed away, their achievements on the field or in the councils of the Colony and State, their heroic endurance from savage and Christian foes—who have by their stately deeds laid broad and deep the foundations of our civil and religious institutions, which should be held in sacred remembrance.

Of our Dutch ancestry in Ulster county, a few are said to have come here to trade with the Esopus Indians as early as 1614. New Amsterdam (now New York) and Fort Orange (now Albany) had a few settlers about the same period : they were traders with the Indians. Settlements were not formed until several years subsequent. In 1695 Miller's History of New York was published in London : there were in it plans of three places of strength, New York, Albany and Kingston, which continued to be the three most important places till 1777. The Dutch ancestry in Ulster county during the greater part of the 17th century were predominant in numbers and influence. By inter-marriages with the Huguenot emigrants and others who fraternized with the Dutch and finally adopted their religion as well as their customs, the line of descent between the Dutch and Huguenots branched out, and the spirit of the Dutch character was blended in common suffering with savage and Christian foes, and had a tendency to increase the bond of friendship, and was attended with most beneficial results.

The character of the Dutch has been conservative, steadfastly adhering to the church of their fathers, living in peace and concord with other denominations. The history of our State shows their spirit of patriotism, adherance to popular rights and civil liberty throughout the Colonial annal and Revolutionary struggle. The tribute paid them by that eminent jurist, Chancellor Kent, in his address before the New York Historical Society, New York, in 1828, will be found characteristic and true.

The Dutch discoverers of New Netherlands were grave, temperate, firm, persevering men, who brought with them the industry, the economy, the simplicity, the integrity and the bravery of their Belgic sires, and with those virtues they also imported the lights of the Roman civil law and the purity of the Protestant faith. To that period we are to look with chastened awe and respect for the beginning of our city and the works of our primitive fathers.

American citizens can never forget the heroic struggle for freedom in England during the period which constituted the transition state from the oppression of the Tudors and Stewarts to the constitutional liberty which they enjoyed under the Commonwealth of England. The close sympathy which was felt by our pilgrim ancestors, Elliot, Hampden, Milton, Vane and Pym, in that struggle against the alleged tyrannical reign of Charles I., the protectorate of Cromwell during the Commonwealth of England, the apparent freedom England then enjoyed, was probably the origin of our national existence, and which planted the institutions of piety and learning on the shores of America. The history of that great man Cromwell, who refused the Crown of England, has yet to be written. The Puritans who emigrated to America were the conservators of civil and religious freedom. The English are an aggressive race; they descended from the Saxons, or more properly speaking, were conquered by the warlike Teutonic tribe, inhabitants of the north-western part of Germany, near the shores of the Baltic. There is reason to believe that the Saxon had formed small colonies there about the same period, and from their intermixture is derived the Anglo-Saxon as applied to the Teutonic race which settled in the southern part of Britain. England is only an abbreviation of Anglo-land or the land of the Angles, by which subsequently the country became known in this early and rude period of England's history.

About two centuries ago many of the Anglo-Saxons emigrated to Ulster county. They were loyal to the Crown until the Revolutionary struggle, when they revolted against her arbitrary and unjust course and espoused the cause of their adopted country against oppression, and aided and contributed to the independence of these United States.

Henry IV. of France issued the edict of Nantes for the protection of the Huguenots, both politically and religiously in 1598.

The Huguenots were the artizans of France. The revocation of the edict of Nantes by Louis XIV, in 1685, the ordinary workmen, who were accustomed to work under the direction of the Huguenots, on their expulsion, caused by the persecutions they encountered, laid the blame of their expulsion on the clergy, which caused their starving condition, having no work nor means for support. Then commenced a series of persecutions against all priests, both Catholic and Protestant, the Bible and its teachings, and all religions were banished from France ; Atheism prevailed. Then followed a frightful scene of disorder, which was then enacted and continued. Robespiere and his followers continued to decapitate the nobles, richer land holders, and then selections were made for victims among the small land holders. Finally they were made among the Commonalty and then commenced the cry, Down with the tyrant Robespiere, and he met an awful death. During the progress of the French revolution, which continued and was brought about by those disorders resulting principally from the effects of the expulsion of the Huguenots, and the results arising from the banishment of the Bible and the overthrow of all religion, and persecution of the priests of all denominations, anarchy followed.

The writer's conclusion from history is that no Republic can stand or continue without the Bible and the Christian religion. If Atheists were the friends of the State they would recommend the Bible and its teachings as essential for the maintenance and support of any free government. The French revolution, of 1789 to 1794, and its awful results, demonstrated most clearly this established fact. The human mind is so constituted, particularly at a period when age causes man to see the necessity of religion of some kind as the only satisfactory solace when the world is receding from their view. The result in revolutionary France was that order was not restored until the collossal power obtained by the conquering sword of Napoleon Bonaparte, who was then swaying the destinies of France, restored the Christian religion and the Bible and its teachings. As a necessary result order and law were again triumphant. This great man knew that such a restoration was necessary for his ambitious aspirations, as he was about ascending the steps of an imperial throne.

After the revocation of the Edict of Nantes, in 1685, this skillful people, who carried on nearly all the manufactures of France, found that their liberties, one after another, were wrested from them, their clergy were forbidden to preach, their teachers to give instruction excepting in writing and arithmetic. Public office and the professions were shut against them and they lost the shelter of the laws. Regiments of Dragoons hunted them down. All this caused the last drop in their cup of bitterness. Shaking the dust of France forever from their feet, 600,000 Huguenots fled with brave hearts and skillful hands to England, Holland and Germany, where they were joyfully received. Many emigrated from Holland to America, where they were received with open arms, and ultimately melted in the general blood of America, who reaped the benefit arising from the manufacturing skill and general intelligence of these Huguenot refugees.

It is a remarkable fact that about the same period William Penn, the purest and most honest among rulers, was rendering his name forever illustrious by establishing in America a refuge for the oppressed from the storms of persecution, and obtained from Charles II. of England a patent to form a settlement in the New World, where the Society of Friends and others might be unmolested, in the Colony of Pennsylvania, at Philadelphia. Louis XIV., one of the most gorgeous and heartless of sovereigns, and one of the most powerful of French monarchs, was about the same period delivering up 300,000 families of his Protestant subjects, the artizans of France, to the atrocious tyranny of the fanatical Le Tellier and the sanguinary Louvois. Louis' great blunder, as a statesman, was his treatment of the Huguenots ; they were the most moral, industrious and intelligent of the French population, and when they were expelled from their native land they enriched England, Holland, Germany and America with the commerce and arts of France.

Ascending the Hudson the Huguenots landed at Wiltwyck (now Kingston), and were welcomed by the Dutch settlers, who had prepared the way in the then wilderness for their enjoyment of civil and religious privileges. The region selected by the Huguenots for their future abode was like their own delightful France. It wanted the culture and improvements of the former, but the picturesque and the sublime in nature appeared on every side. Running streams, verdant lawns, hills, and woods charmed the eye. Toward the east the charming prospect was bounded by the noble and ever rolling Hudson. The lofty Catskills delighted their vision while at Kingston, where they remained about fifteen years before leaving for New Paltz, about 1683, where they remained as their final resting place. The Shawangunk and the Fishkill range of mountains gave additional beauty to the scene. The Rosendale begins its course far in the interior, and uniting with the Wallkill then rapidly passes on till it unites with the Hudson. So with the Esopus creek ; its source is among the mountains of the Delaware, whence it rushes furiously onward until it reaches Marbletown : from thence it runs northerly until it mingles with the Hudson at Saugerties, Ulster county. About twenty families remained at Kingston. The Dutch and French Huguenots followed these noble streams. Their descendants now enjoy the rich and glorious patrimony secured by the industry, frugality and piety of their ancestors.

The county of Ulster is considerably broken by those lofty monarchs of the Hudson, the Catskills. Numerous little streams and creeks enrich this beautiful region not far from Kingston. New Paltz being the principal homes of these Huguenots a patent was obtained for the lands from Colonial Governor Andros ; they selected twelve of their brethren as the patentees, who are known by the appellation of the twelve patentees. A list of the original purchasers were : Louis DuBois, Christian Deyo, Abraham Hasbrouck, Andres Lefevre, John Brook (said to have been changed to Hasbrouck), Peter Dean (or Deyo), Louis Bevier, Anthony Crispell, Abraham DuBois, Hugh Freer, Isaac DuBois, Simon Lefevre.

A copy of this treaty with the Indians exists, and was executed May 26, 1677. They were three days on their journey from Kingston to New Paltz. Soon, however, they selected a more elevated site upon the banks of the beautiful Wallkill, where the ancient village now stands. Kingston was then their only trading village.

The French church, of which Louis DuBois was the first elder, was established in 1683. For 50 years the language they used was French : subsequently for 70 years succeeded by the Low Dutch : since the beginning of the 19th century English has been their church vernacular.

Rev. Mr. Dallie, from New York, visited New Paltz January 26, 1683, and occasionally conducted services for them. Their then house of worship was a stone edifice, where they worshipped 81 years, when it was demolished in 1839. The Huguenots finally by intermarriages and intercourse with the Dutch adopted their language, manners and customs, and finally gave up their French church and accepted and joined with the Reformed Dutch denomination, and worshipped with the Dutch in the same church edifice.

The Irish settled in Esopus (now Kingston) at an early period : many of them were men of wealth and standing. This useful class of citizens, many of whom are connected with the public works, are engaged in the stone, lime, cement, real estate and railroad employments. They are generous-hearted and impulsive. As men of toil they have been of vast service in developing the resources of this county (the writer is speaking of them only as inhabitants of Ulster county), whose chief city is Kingston. They have advanced this county by their efforts in peace and in war : they are always ready to fight the battles of our country, and are loyal and ready to protect its flag—the emblem of its power—against any daring invader, and to support and protect the interests and independence of our country.

The writer states that he has endeavored to give short sketches of the lives of the most prominent men of the seventeenth and eighteenth centuries and only a few of a later period : the limits of the work prevent him from including many others.

The history of the First Reformed Dutch Church of Kingston, organized in 1659—first clergyman called was Rev. Harmanus Blom, who commenced this pastorate September, 1660—is so full of interest a brief statement thereof will be inserted. Its several pastors in the order of succession from 1659 to 1883 are as follows : Laurentius Van Gaasbeck, successor to Blom, from 1667 to 1680 ; then follow Johannes Weekstein, Laurentius Van der Bock, I. P. Nucella, Francis L. Beys, Peter Vas, George Wilhelm Mancius, Dr. Harmanus Meyer, Dr. George I. L. Doll, the last of the Dutch ministers educated in the Universities of Holland : this eminent man's pastorate commenced in the year 1775 and continued till the year 1808. During the troublesome and stormy period of the American Revolution his heroic bearing and patriotic services rendered in support of the new State of New York and its first illustrious Governor, George Clinton, are recorded in history, which perpetuates the memory of this eminent divine.

Dr. John Gossman was the successor of Rev. Dr. Doll ; then follow Dr. John Lillie, I. W. Van Wagonen, Dr. John C. F. Hoes, Dr. D. W. Vanderveer, and the present pastor, Dr. J. G. Van Slyke.

Rev. Dr. John Gossman was born February 10, 1784, and was called to this church in the year 1808 : his pastorate continued till about the year 1835. He was distinguished as an eminent divine, possessed of a powerful, rich and melodious voice, and was one of the most popular preachers of his day. He departed this life December 8, 1865.

Rev. Dr. John C. F. Hoes, born in 1811, was called to this church in 1845 : his pastorate continued for 21 years, till the year 1866, when he resigned, and continued to reside in Kingston till his death, distinguished as a sound and able dominie, dignified in his deportment, honest and unflinching in discharging the duties of his high calling. He officiated for neighboring congregations frequently till his death with great acceptance in the county where he so long resided. His valuable paper read by him at the Kingston Centennial, July 30, 1877, relative to the venerable church where he so long officiated as pastor, correspondence of Dr. Doll with Governor Clinton in 1777, relative to the destruction of the church building standing in that year, his *fac simile* furnished of the signatures of all the ministers of this church from Rev. Mr. Blom to and including Dr. Van Slyke, all set forth in the history of Ulster county, are valuable contributions which every friend of the church ought to preserve.

He suddenly left the presence of his family and numerous friends, who deeply mourned their loss, at Kingston, about June, 1883. The community where he so long resided hearing of his sudden departure, joined his afflicted family and friends in sorrow for their loss and respect for his memory. His widow and two daughters and only son Rev. Randall Hoes, chaplain in the U. S. Navy, constitute his surviving family.

An interesting sketch of the First Reformed Dutch Church at Kingston, N. Y., which is copied from the December number of the *Magazine of the Reformed Dutch Church*, published in the year 1826, more than 56 years ago, as follows :

[For the Dutch Church Magazine.]

KINGSTON CHURCH, 1826.

The village of Kingston had a settled minister as early as the year 1662 : being more than forty-eight years after the first landing here, of the emigrants from Holland. The hamlet at that time was called Wildwyck, or Indian district : and afterward Esopus. The first clergyman was the Rev. Hermanus Blom, whose accounts for salary, *all payable in wheat*, are preserved to this day, in the county records. He preached in a log hut, on the site of the present building. Yet, even in that rude edifice reared by the piety of our ancestors, God condescended to meet and to bless us. The second Church building was in the ancient style ornamented with highly coloured, painted, and burnt window glass, bearing the coat of arms of our progenitors from Vanderland. The third was a larger building, erected in 1752, as appears by the names of the workmen, and the year of their labours, cut in hewn stone, and masoned into the front wall of the present building. The fourth and last structure is of blue limestone, with a lofty tower of the same materials, in which hangs a Holland bell, imported from Amsterdam in 1794 : which measures seven feet six inches in circumference at its mouth ; is two feet two inches in height, and is remarkable for its clear and deep-toned peals. This was the first bell that ever tolled here for a funeral : the previous usage having been to ring the bell on such occasions. It was also the practice before this time to ring the bell three times a day by way of notice, to tidy house-keepers, of their breakfast, dinner and supper hours.

At present the town clock regulates the kitchen. The bell was also formerly rung whenever there was a baptism, or a *christening* as it was called : and then the minister, with an elder, and whoever else pleased, went into Church, and performed the rites of baptism. On the top of the steeple is an iron cross, fastened horizontally according to the magnetic meridian : and accurately designating the four cardinal points of the compass. This was in former days surmounted by a large cock; which, they say, was the memento of Peter's denial of his Master. And on the top of the pulpit was Noah's dove holding the olive branch in her mouth : but these emblems of those feathered worthies, have also mingled in the rubbish of oblivion. There was, also, until demolished within a few years, a Consistory-house, built in front of the Church door, according to the fashion of the Dutch Churches generally. This appendage was not erected until 1721, as appears by a stone tablet, saved from the ruins, and imbedded in the front wall of the present building, inscribed P. VAS. MDCCXXI. The first bell used by the Church, was a present from Captain Anthony Rutgers, of the city of New-York : and is the same bell now mounted in the cupola of the new court-house. The present Church bell was also procured from Holland, through the agency of Captain Rutgers ; a name dear to Kingston and to the Dutch Church. It was also the custom among our forefathers, immediately before the ringing of the last bell for Church service, to be notified by a rap at each door, from the ivory-headed cane of the grey-headed sexton, who sung out aloud, "*church time:*" and for this circuit, was paid by each family two shillings per annum. The sexton also carried to the clerk, all written requests for the prayers of the congregation. The clerk had a long rod, slit at the end, into which he stuck the note, and handed it up to the minister : who, in those days occupied a very high pulpit in the shape of a half globe, raised on the top of a demi column : and canopied with a sounding board. The knob for the Minister's hat, exhibited a likeness of the president of the American Congress of 1777, with his name underneath " Laurens : " thus uniting patriotism with devotion. The minister wore a black silk mantle, a cocked hat, and a neckband with linen cambrick " *belly*" on his breast ; for *cravats* were then *uncanonical.* The first psalm used to be set with movable figures suspended on three sides of the pulpit : so that every one as they entered, might prepare for the lofty notes : which in those days were printed with each psalm : and it was deemed an accomplishment to dwell long and loud on a *mi, fa, sol.* And, to give them an ague-like shake, in those days of primeval simplicity : the deacons, when service was ended, rose in their places, the pastor distilled on them the dew of charity, in a short address : they bowed, took each a bag fixed to a long black pole, with a small *alarm* bell fastened to the end, went their rounds, steering clear of the canopy, the pillars, and the bonnets ; and rousing the sleepy heads with experienced dexterity, and returned heavy laden with farthings : or, with a copper coin called *tokens,* being stamped with " Kingston Church," and redeemed at stated times. Nor is it less worthy of notice in our precise ancestors, that they never approached a communion table, unless apparelled in black : a sort of silent language, saying, " Do this in remembrance of me." It was then also usual to stand round the sacramental board, which was placed at the foot of the pulpit. Instead of exhortations from the Minister, after he had broken the bread and handed the cup, the clerk read aloud a suitable chapter from the Prophet Isaiah, or John the Evangelist. The clerk also read a portion of Scripture, before the Minister came into

Church, in order to withdraw the minds of the congregation from worldly matters. There was a canopied seat expressly set apart for the county clerk, the sheriff, and the town magistrates : and also a separate bench for the trustees of the corporation. The rest of the seats were held, not in pews, but as single seats promiscuously ; and, at the death of the occupant, were again " booked " for life, to the next of kin ; or, on their neglect, to the first applicant.

Until the year 1808, Kingston Church stood alone as an independent Church ; and having been so for a century and a half, it threw an air of superiority around her, which was not easily subdued by the regular judicatories of the Dutch Church in America. A great consistory had once been called, and had rejected the jurisdiction of the General Synod. Our clergy were ordained in Europe, and we had received an ample charter, granted to us by the British Crown, November 17, 1719, which gave us full powers to conduct our internal affairs. But it was at last thought, that, as the English language had nearly supplanted the Dutch ; and, as it would therefore, be useless to send to Holland for our Ministers, we might rather unite with the ecclesiastical associations at our doors. Another great consistory was accordingly called September 5, 1808 ; and out of twenty-eight members only four voted against joining the Synod. Then we gave the hand of fellowship to our sister Churches. And, although our sturdy notions of independence at first caused many billows of trouble to roll over us, yet are we now at peace ; and we leave the records of our public charities to speak their own eulogy.

Eleven clergymen have been settled in this Church from its first planting in the new world, to this time, viz :

Blom, Van Gaasbeek, Weekstein, Nucella, Van Bosen, Beys, Vas, Mancius, Meyer, Doll, Gosman.

Of these, the Rev. P. Vas died here at ninety-six years of age, and his great-grandchild and other descendants are now living in this village.

The Rev. W. Mancius also died here, and is buried within the walls of the Church. The Rev. Mr. Meyer died in New Jersey. The Rev. G. Doll, at the age of seventy-two, died, and was interred at Kinderhook. A half length portrait and true likeness of this good man, was taken by Vanderlyn, and is preserved in Kingston as a memorial to his numerous friends. The remains of his deceased consort Mrs. Doll, are also entombed within the Church.

Among the descendants of these clergymen, are the daughter of Dominie Mancius, and the great-grandson of Dominie Vas ; both of whom first partook of the Lord's supper in this Church, sixty-six years ago ; and are yet among the regular attendants at the communion table.

A stranger merely passing the burying ground, would be apt to think there had been great mortality here, from the number of graves and gravestones. But on looking at the inscriptions, he will find some to exceed one hundred years. At the head of one grave stands a cedar post and a stone slab chiselled with the year 1710. Yet this post is solid, and when chipped with a knife, has the odor peculiar to that kind of wood. On the subject of mortality it may be stated with certainty, that by the census of last year the population of the compact part of the village is 1170 ; and for the last twelve months the births were 31, and the deaths only 15. Let me add one

more, and a highly gratifying statistical fact. This congregation embraces 1700 souls : of these 328 are communicants : and of that number 240 have been added to the Church during the pastoral charge of the Rev. Mr. Gosman ; a proof that he is "a burning and a shining light in the ministry."
June, 1826.   BOERHAAVE.

A friend of the writer, Cornelius Van Gassbeek, Esq., for many years an elder, and prominent in the First Reformed Dutch Church at Kingston, has a diploma of his ancestor Rev. Laurentius Van Gaasbeek, second pastor of said church, received from the University of Lyden, Holland, where he graduated May 24, 1674. Also has an old oil painting of Rev. Johannes. Weekstein, third pastor of said church. Date on said painting, 1674.

CITY OF KINGSTON.

—◆—

The following articles relating to Kingston's history, growth, industries, &c., published in the Kingston *Daily Freeman* of June 23d and 30th, 1883, are so immediately connected with the foregoing that writer has concluded to reprint the same, as follows:

EARLY FACTS CONCERNING KINGSTON.

The Men Who Founded It—Wars and Politics—Religious Interests—Public and Private Buildings—The Prospect Twelve Years Ago.

Editor Freeman :—In 1871 I wrote the following article which was then published in the *Christian Intelligencer* of New York, and republished in Kingston papers. At the time it was received with much favor, but as I was unable to furnish the great demand for papers containing the article, I now propose to offer the same for republication, preliminary to another article showing the changes that have since taken place, entitled : "City of Kingston, its Mountain Hotels, Railroads, Industries and Commercial Prosperity," indicative of its becoming what nature and the enterprise of a few citizens intended it to be—the foremost commercial city between New York and Albany.   FREDERICK E. WESTBROOK.

Kingston and its Overlook Mountain House.

Kingston, formerly known as Atkarkarton, Wiltwyck and Esopus, had a few settlers who located among the Esopus Indians in 1614.

Rev. I. Megapolensis, third minister of the Collegiate Dutch Church of New York, in a letter on the state of religion in the province of New York, to the classis of Amsterdam, dated August 5, 1657, says : " Thomas Chambers and a few others removed to Atkarkarton, or Esopus (now Kingston), an exceedingly beautiful land, in 1652, and began the actual settlement of Ulster county ; it was also known among the savages as the Pleasant Land."

From the date of the first settling of this place, the following are the names of the Director-Generals of the province of New York, sent out from Holland : Andrisen Jores, whose administration commenced in 1623 ; Cornelius Jacobsen May, William Verhulst, Peter Minuit, under whose administration, in 1626, Manhattan Island (New York), was purchased from the Indians for $24. Then follow Wouter Van Twiller, William Kieft, and last, the valiant, energetic, able and faithful Petrus Stuyvesant, whose administration commenced May 11, 1647, in whom the early settlers of Kingston, long harrassed by the savages, found a powerful friend.

The wars with the Indians and negotiations and troubles with his English neighbors continued till New Amsterdam surrendered to the English in 1664, when Stuyvesant (released from the vexations and turmoils of public life), after visiting Holland, returned to New York, and spent the rest of his days in retirement on his "Bowerie," where he departed his laborious and useful life in 1671. Under the administration of William Kieft, Rev. Evardus Bogardus, the first minister (and Adam Roelandson, the first schoolmaster) arrived in the colony, and officiated at New Amsterdam, in the Collegiate Reformed Church, from 1633 to 1647. He married the widow of Roeloff Jansen, who was then called Anneke Jans, or Roeloff, and had four children by her former husband, and after her marriage with the Dominie she had four children. The farm, about which so much money has been wasted in litigation, contained sixty-two acres, now of immense value —which land was granted to Roeloff Jansen in 1636. Upon his death it passed to his widow and heirs; it went subsequently by the name of the "Dominie's Bowerie." After his death, in 1647, being lost at sea, his widow resided in New York, and in 1654 the grant of the farm was confirmed to her and her heirs by Director-General Stuyvesant, and subsequently confirmed by the English government. Her heirs disposed of this property to Col. Francis Lovelace, then Governor of New York. One of her sons, Cornelius, did not join in the conveyance, and it has been alleged that his heirs are entitled to a share in this vast property. In 1705 the farm (then called King's Farm) was leased by the colonial authorities to Trinity church, New York. The object of this statement is to assure the numerous alleged heirs residing at Kingston and vicinity, that it is an act of folly to pay lawyers for the recovery of this property, which is barred by the statute of limitations; there is no earthly hope of success, and if the writer's advice is taken the object of this statement is accomplished.

Dominie Blom, first minister at Wiltwyck (now Kingston), arrived from Holland and commenced his pastoral duties (as first minister) with sixteen members, May 12, 1660. Much might be said of this remarkable man. A work is soon to be published, being a history of the Dutch clergymen of Kingston, by a prominent minister, Rev. Dr. Hoes, which I am told will include an interesting sketch of the early history of this place. Constant depredations and loss of life occurred in disputes with the Indians during the whole of Stuyvesant's administration, and he frequently visited this place to quell those disturbances. His advice to the farmers of Wiltwyck (now Kingston) was, for their security from the savages, to form a village, which they at first strenuously opposed, but subsequently acceeded to, and during Stuyvesant's sojourn the site of the present village was selected, and the work was commenced May 31, 1658, and while engaged in building and stockading the same the savages appeared, not with hostile intentions, but to present the site of the village to the Grand Sachem Stuyvesant as a present to grease his feet, as he had taken so long and painful a journey to visit them (more properly to chastise them). A charter was obtained May 16, 1661, municipal powers were first granted, and the village was called Wiltwyck, or Indian village, as it was a present from the savages. Evart Pels, Cornelius Barentson Sleight and Elbert Heyman Rosa were appointed *schopens*, and Roeloff Swartwout, *schout*. A frightful and memorable massacre occurred at this place by the Indians June 7th, 1663. After great loss of life and a partial destruction of their village, the savages were finally driven out by the exertions of Thomas Chambers, Swartwout, and the valiant Dominie Blom. The latter has given a detail of this awful event. Thomas Chambers, first settler of Wiltwyck (now Kingston), was the recipient of an order issued by Governor Lovelace, dated October 16th, 1672, setting forth that Capt. Thomas Chambers, Justice at Esopus, hath done signal service in the time of the Indian wars, and having a house not far from Kingston, and in acknowledgment of his services, the said house was erected into the Manor of Foxhall. This grant was confirmed in October, 1686, by Governor Dongan. With all these temporal honors, he had no children. His first wife was Margaretta Hendricks. He subsequently, the writer believes, married the widow of Rev. Laurentius VanGaasbeek, whose son assumed the name of Abraham VanGaasbeck Chambers, and became heir to the Manor of Foxhall on the death of his stepfather in 1696. The name of Foxhall has now disappeared except from the Book of Patents. The widow of Thomas Chambers, on his death, married Col. Wessel TenBroeck, before mentioned, prominent at that period, and who was the great ancestor of the TenBroeck and VanGaasbeck families of this place. William Beekman was Sheriff of Kingston until the close of Governor Lovelace's administration in 1674, when he returned to New York. He was born at Hasselt, in Overrysel, in 1623, emigrated to America, and died in New York in 1707, with distinguished reputation, filling many official positions. The present William and Beekman streets, New York, bear his name. He married Catharine Deboogh, and had several children. His eldest daughter married a son of Governor Stuyvesant. Henry, his eldest son, settled at Kingston ; was Judge of Ulster county and member of the Provincial Legislature. His daughter Margaret married Robert R. Livingston, and among her children were Janet, wife of the late Richard Montgomery, who fell at the siege of Quebec, and the late Chancellor Robert R. Livingston. These brief facts are fully set forth in Brodhead's, O'Callagan's, Miller's, Dunlap's, McAuley's and Valentine's histories of New York.

Among the prominent stone buildings now standing, which have survived the burning of Kingston, in 1777, and which were repaired after the Revolution, are the Hasbrouck Mansion, residence of Hon. A. Bruyn Hasbrouck, ex-President of Rutger's College ; the old Academy, where many prominent men of the seventeenth century received their preparatory education : the Schoonmaker Mansion, owned by Hon. M. Schoonmaker ; the Beckman House, late residence of Mrs. Rachel Beckman, a remarkable woman in her day, who died in her 94th year, and who has related to the writer interesting events at the burning of Kingston by the British : and the TenBroeck Mansion, corner of North Front street and Clinton avenue, erected by Col. Wessel TenBroeck about the year 1676. General Armstrong (who married a sister of the late Chancellor Livingston), Secretary of War, occupied this house until 1804, when he left for France, Minister to that court. The late Rev. Dr. C. D. Westbrook resided here till his death, in 1858. The Senate of the State of New York was held in this building in 1777, the year of the adoption of its first constitution.

Modern Kingston was incorporated in 1805. It is beautifully located, about one hundred and eighty feet above the level of the sea, on an extensive plain, surrounded by distant and near mountain scenery, extensive views of the lowlands, where runs the Kingston Creek, a rapid mountain stream which empties into the Hudson at Saugerties. Washington Irving was an admirer of the magnificent scenery at this place, who, as he surveyed the Catskill Mountains, in company with ex-President VanBuren and General Smith, of Kingston, exclaimed, " This is the most impressive and beautiful mountain scenery that I have ever witnessed." The health of this place is well known, as persons known to the writer, former residents of New York and Brooklyn, are residing here for benefit from disease of the lungs, and experience much relief. Its beautiful churches (the First Reformed is one of the most beautiful in the State), Presbyterians, Episcopalians, Baptists and Methodists have fine edifices. The Second Reformed church, erected in 1850, a beautiful and costly edifice, which was shortly after its erection embarrassed, was saved by the timely liberality of the Collegiate Church of New York, through the efforts of the Consistory, and efficient aid given to their application by the late Rev. Dr. C. D. Westbrook. It is now out of debt, and has a wealthy and powerful congregation, under the able ministry of Dr. Stitt, the present pastor. The intelligence, social habits, and refinements of its citizens render this place a delightful residence for those who are desirous of being released from active business and the excitement and vexations incident to city life. Kingston, besides being a pleasant residence not surpassed by any village in this

State, is in a flourishing condition. The population of the town of Kingston, including Rondout, in 1840 was 5,800 : in 1870 it increased to 21,000. The population of Ulster county in 1840 was 39,000, and in 1870, 84,000 —a ratio of increase exceeded by only a few places. The Delaware and Hudson Canal, the Rondout and Oswego Railroad, the Wallkill Valley Railroad, from New York, terminating at Kingston December next, and a railroad to connect with Rondout and Oswego to Boston, via the Connecticut Western, is in progress. The stone trade of the county is said to amount to $4,000,000 annually, and its lime and cement works are powerful agencies at work in giving an increasing business character to this place, which is soon to become, with Rondout, a large city, separated by the distance of one mile, to which it is united by a horse railroad.

The Overlook Mountain Company of Kingston have recently completed a Mountain House on one of the highest peaks of the Catskills, said to accommodate three hundred guests, and is in every respect a first-class hotel, kept by Mr. Lasher, whose reputation is well established. I would advise all who have an interest in mountain scenery to visit this interesting place, said to be 3,800 feet in height, and which overlooks many points of interest that cannot be seen at any other place in the Catskill Mountains.

On the ever-memorable 12th of July last, the writer was one among a large party from Kingston and Rondout who visited this mountain house. It was a joyous and happy occasion of meeting many familiar faces and prominent and well-known citizens. Early in the morning, the lowering clouds, indicative of a storm, did not prevent this party from assembling in large numbers at the depot of the Rondout and Oswego Railroad : it was intended as a deserved compliment to the enterprise of the company (of which Mr. Artemas Sahler, a prominent merchant of Kingston, is President), and to the proprietor, Mr. Lasher (who is said to have expended $25,000 in furnishing and adorning this place), and to cheer onward by the presence of so many of its friends an undertaking which, in connection with a project now maturing for the erection, by a joint stock company, of a large, first-class hotel at Kingston for summer boarders, to accommodate three hundred guests, and intended to co-operate with its Mountain House, which, when completed, the success of the Mountain House will exceed the anticipations of its founders. To return to our party : toward noon the morning clouds dispersed and the brilliant orb of day shone in unusual splendor. The scene before us was magnificent. To the east the well-known Round Top appeared on a level with us. The westerly view of the Catskills was the subject of much remark ; it was a point of surpassing beauty. The celebrated Paltz Point, a place of great resort, was noticed as an elevated hill : apparently we could discover the cultivated plains beyond, looking over the

3

Point. The most distant view north was above Albany, and on the south, near New York, and many other attractive points of interest in this elevated position and temperature of refreshing coolness, might be presented to the reader. The eye of the visitor gazes long upon the wide expanse of lovely and sublime scenery, spending hours in surveying the various points of interest. We had the pleasure of witnessing the beauty of the setting sun beyond the dark outlines of the distant mountains, which was only surpassed by the splendor of its rising on the following cloudless morning. During the evening the spacious parlors were filled; the music of the Rondout Band, and the social qualifications of our party, and pleasant conversation relative to the scenes of the day, caused all to be cheerful and happy. At 4 o'clock on the following afternoon many of our party returned to Kingston, where we arrived at 6 P. M. The view from the summit of Overlook is not exceeded in grandeur, beauty and extent of its natural and cultivated scenery by any other mountain top. The writer has visited the tops of Mount Washington and Mansfield during sunshine and storm; while impressed with the vastness and extent of the mountain-tops of the former, and the beauty of the cultivated scenery of the latter, yet nothing seems to surpass the varied and indescribable beauties of mountain and cultivated scenery as seen from Overlook.   F. E. W.

New York, August, 1871.

KINGSTON'S INDUSTRIES AND PROGRESS.

Its Churches, Schools, Steamboats, Railroads, Coal Trade and Manufacturing Establishments—Its Present and Future Greatness.

Editor Freeman :—On this auspicious and memorable occasion (25th day of June, 1883), all nature smiles, and is glowing in luxuriant early summer beauty, adorning the varied and magnificent scenery with its lofty Catskills, which at no other place than Kingston appear so grand, sublime and attractive to the beholder. The bounteous harvest which Providence is about to provide, all conspire to gladden and cheer the pathway, and to elevate the minds of the large numbers of Kingston's most prominent citizens, assembled at the Union Depot of the New York, West Shore and Buffalo Railroad to witness the important event of the departure of its first train of cars to New York, which was celebrated by the firing of cannon, and ringing of church bells, a splendid band of music giving additional interest to the fairy scene. On the return of the cars in the evening the excitement of the morning was greatly increased, the number of citizens assembled was about 4,000 : the fireworks and other expenses were incurred by the merchants uptown, who are ever ready to appreciate such an important event. This unexpected and great demonstration is indicative that the people understand the benefits arising from a great trunk line of railroad passing through, equi-distant from both sections of this beautiful and historical city. This road is the port of upper Kingston during twelve months of each year, and settles forever the vexed question relative to the supremacy of either section. Upper Kingston's continued growth and power are now permanently established. Both sections can now enter upon a career of prosperity accelerated by the completion of its important public works. Having no railroads in her rear, and owing to the configuration of its mountains, this city is forever protected from such a calamity as has befallen its sister cities. Its coal, limestone, cement, brick, carriage factories, foundries and other varied industries, and the minerals to be obtained from the bowels of the earth, amounting to millions annually, as will be hereafter set forth, are inducements sufficient for its citizens of both sections to enter now upon a new order of things, and the only sectional feeling hereafter should be the laudable one which will contribute most for the general prosperity of all.

The completion of the West Shore Railroad to Kingston is the crowning glory of the several railroads now in successful operation to this place, one of which has been extended, and its first train of cars has commenced running this 25th day of June, 1883, from Tannersville Junction to the Kaaterskill and Beach's old mountain house, the depot of which is at Catskill Lake, one-half mile distant therefrom. These several railroads will be briefly set forth. The Wallkill Valley, lately foreclosed, was purchased by Kingston's distinguished capitalist, Hon. Thomas Cornell, who after a great outlay of money and labor put the same in complete running order, and disposed of it lately to the West Shore and Buffalo Railroad. The bonding of the Rondout and Oswego Railroad, now known as the Ulster and Delaware, and its subsequent foreclosure and purchase by Hon. Thomas Cornell, are events too widely known to discuss. The effect of this foreclosure and bonding was to enable him to purchase the same and put it in complete order with steel rails, etc., running now to Stamford, its passenger and freight list doubling every short period. Without this bonding and foreclosure Mr. Cornell certainly would never have purchased the same. The argument has been advanced that the bonding of this road and partial completion caused the loss of the wagon trade from Delaware county, and it probably did for a time, which is freely admitted, and which all good citizens regretted. The day had, however, arrived when railroads in this important place were to supercede the wagon business. If Mr. Cornell had not purchased this road, the result would have been a struggle between this city and Catskill which should build this road to Delaware county, which is equi-distant from both. In either event the Kingston wagon trade would inevitably have been superceded. All good citizens are gradually becoming reconciled, and I think will admit that the advent of railroads for the reasons set forth was a matter of necessity. The principal ownership of the Ulster and Delware road happily is in the hands of Mr. Cornell, of which he is President, and is in successful operation, with constantly greatly increased passenger and freight traffic, which has induced that sagacious, enterprising and energetic citizen, S. D. Coykendall, to build and equip the Stony Clove Railroad through a mountain pass to Hunter and Tannersville Junction, on his own responsibility. This important road (Mr. Coykendall being the President thereof), requiring great engineering skill in its construction through an almost inaccessible narrow gorge between elevated mountains, forms a notch in the mountains, and as you approach Hunter the scenery that presents itself is of remarkable beauty and sublimity. Hunter and its vicinity is a great boarding region. Thousands of summer boarders have for years invaded this mountain region of unsurpassed loveliness and beauty. The writer was among a large number of invited guests, a few months ago, that attended the celebration of the completion of the Stony Clove road to Hunter. It was an elegant day, and the ride through the Clove was one of great interest, and on our arrival at Hunter we were all struck with the great display of flags and other decorations. After hearing speeches by Mr. Harding, General Sharpe and others as to the advantages Hunter and Kingston would derive from this great event of building and completing this road, and partaking of an elegant supper prepared by the citizens of Hunter, we returned and reached Kingston at 12 P. M., satisfied that a bond of fraternal union exists between Hunter and Kingston.

A few months after this celebration Hon. Thomas Cornell commenced the Kaaterskill Railroad (of which he is the President), connecting Hunter with Harding's, or the Kaaterskill Hotel, and the old Mountain House, which was completed and opened on this memorable day, the 25th of June, 1883. This new mountain railroad is one of the grand enterprises of the year, is a fitting monument to individual enterprise, and will be appreciated by thousands of summer travellers, who will enjoy all-rail traveling from New York via Kingston to the Harding or Kaaterskill House, which can accommodate 1,000 guests, and several thousand more that occupy the boarding houses from Hunter to said mountain houses. This statement is made as an act of justice to Kingston's all-rail route from New York via Kingston to the Kaaterskill Lake, among and above the clouds, half a mile equi-distant from Beach's old mountain house and Harding's, or Kaaterskill Mountain House.

Wonderful results have been accomplished since 1871. Twelve years ago Kingston was rejoicing over the successful building of the Overlook Mountain House, anticipating it as a great event and a great blessing, together with a few small boarding places constituting all the accommodations in the mountains then accessible via Kingston. In 1883 Kingston is delighted in having the Grand Hotel, Overlook, Kaaterskill Hotel, Laurel House, Kaaterskill Falls, Tremper House, Guigou House, Hunter Hotel, and several other large hotels, and is the gateway by all-rail road from Kingston to nearly 1,000 hotels and boarding places in all parts of the Catskills. Carriage roads have been built by Messrs. Kiersted, connecting Overlook north with Harding's and Beach's mountain houses, and in fact connecting all leading hotels, which increases the variety, enables guests to ride and visit from one prominent hotel to another, and relieves the monotony during their stay. Who can estimate the commercial advantages to Kingston to be derived from the completion of these great public works ? Who can estimate the gratitude due to those prominent citizens, Hon. Thomas Cornell and Mr. S. D. Coykendall, for the solid and enduring benefits they have conferred in the completion of these works ? The eminent men that rear their own monuments by the efforts of their energies, skill, cost and labor, directed for the public welfare, to construct the same successfully, to survive either stone or marble, must be composed of no common material. The annals of this city will record their deeds, and posterity will long continue to enjoy the beneficial results arising from the wisdom displayed in their public services.

This mountain traffic and travel will be a source of wealth and power to this city. It is now in its infancy, and when arriving at the manhood of its strength, will prove a great blessing in opening this important and rich section of country, including Hunter, Delaware county and beyond, to Kingston. A profound sense of gratitude now exists towards those eminent capitalists, not only in this city, but by thousands of summer boarders and others elsewhere, who are so greatly benefitted by their munificent outlays and far-reaching and lasting results arising therefrom. The merchants of the upper section of the city, seeing the importance of this mountain trade, including Hunter and vicinity, and Delaware county, contributed largely to the extension of Fair street to the Ulster and Delaware Railroad, and erected thereon a depot at this point convenient to the business of the upper section in order to share with its lower section in the advantages of its trade, etc. Being in operation over a year these enlightened business men have or will be amply compensated for their generous course of action.

Kingston was organized and incorporated as a city in 1872, governed by a Mayor and eighteen aldermen. The general measures and workings of the city government have been on the whole satisfactory. A reduction of the city funded debt and reduction of taxation have been accomplished, while many public works of utility have been laid out and completed. The ordinary expenses of the city for all general purposes, exclusive of schools, last year amounted to $32,000. The average during the last five years has been about $30,000. In the annual appropriations during said years there has been a small surplus each year.

Union avenue, Wall street, Fair street and Albany avenue have been paved, and has resulted in increasing facilities and beautifying and adding to the value of the property improved. The Kingston water works are in progress. Kingston has now recovered from the effects of the disastrous revulsion and panic which lasted several years, from 1871 to 1878 or 1879, causing a stoppage of public works. There was during that period a surplus of houses. Being a commercial place, few cities felt more seriously the result thereof, which shows more clearly the importance of the place, for at this period (1883) the public and private works are in operation on a large and more extended scale. The completion of the railroads has caused a great demand for dwellings and parts thereof. There are many boarding, unable to find a residence. Kingston is eighty-eight miles from New York, on the north side of Rondout creek, which is navigable for three miles ; population estimated 18,000. It is the terminus of the Delaware and Hudson Canal, which last year brought to tide water 1,300,000 tons of coal, besides an immense tonage of lime, cement, lumber, grain and agricultural products. It has forty steamboats, thirty of which, including the Mary Powell, belong to Cornell Steamboat and Transportation Company. The elegant steamers James W. Baldwin, M. Martin and Eagle, belong to Messrs. Romer & Tremper Steam Transportation Company, of Kingston. It has a wharfage front of four miles, and vessels arrive and depart daily from this port to all parts of the United States with cement, lime, coal, lumber, stone, brick, etc. The tonnage of coal, blue stone, ice, lime and cement, lumber and brick shipped from this port amounts to 2,700,000 tons annually. In a debate a few years ago in the Legislature of this State, it was announced that the tonnage of this city exceeded that of the city of Albany.

Kingston is the centre of the blue stone and flagging business, which is scattered through a section nearly ninety miles in length, reaching from near Delaware river to the Hudson. This is brought to this city by wagon, rail and canal. Among the prominent stone dealers are William B. Fitch, Noone & Madden, Sweeny Brothers, Daniel E. Donovan, Booth & Moran, H. Boice, J. V. Cummings. Noone & Madden furnished 250,000 tons of stone for the abutment of Brooklyn and New York bridge, also large quantities for Erie Canal enlargement, Government lighthouses, etc., which require stone of solidity and durability, and is considered superior for such purposes to granite obtained from other sections. This firm's monthly payments, when on contract work, exceed $10,000 per month. The largest cement manufactory in this city is the Newark Lime and Cement Works, which turned out last year 243,000 barrels. The cement is obtained by tunneling the hills which face the Rondout creek, and running galleries in the layers of rock. These galleries are nearly two miles in length and are often sunk to the depth of 200 feet. The average thickness of the layers is thirty feet and incline to all angles. Hon. James G. Lindsley, first Mayor of this city, is the general manager.

The Hudson River Lime and Cement Works, Mr. E. M. Brigham general manager, turns out about 150,000 barrels annually. The Lawrenceville Lime and Cement Works, of which the late Mr. Beach, of New York (deceased), was President ; these works are very extensive. He departed this life a few months ago, and was much respected in this city. Norton's cement works are very large and extensive. Time and space will not permit me further to enlarge and speak of the large number engaged in the trade. From the best information I can obtain (from Mr. Lindsley and other sources), the annual amount of cement shipped from this port amounts to 1,500,000 tons. Other estimates may exceed that number.

This city also contains four foundries and six machine shops and steam engine builders, two planing mills, one manufactory of malt, eighteen of cigars, one of glue, three tanneries, two of tombstones and monuments, nine breweries, thirteen carriage manufactories, six sash and blind factories, three blue stone rubbing and polishing mills, one butter tub factory. The principal lumber and manufacturing yards are Burhans & Felten, Howard Osterhoudt, Overbaugh & Turner, Wm. J. Turck, H. W. Palen, and others. Newspaper and printing, *Freeman* Job Printing Establishment, Kingston *Argus, Kingston Daily Freeman, Kingston Journal and Weekly Freeman,* the *Daily* and *Weekly Leader,* and J. P. Hageman, job printer. John D. Sleight, Tracy N. Stebbins, George L. Wachmeyer, and Stock & Rice are the most prominent manufacturers and dealers in furniture. Crosby, Sahler & Co., Winne, Payntar, and A. & J. Hasbrouck are heavy dealers and manufacturers of hardware. The business of these several manufacturing firms is simply immense, including the several firms in the dry goods trade, where articles of luxury of every variety can be obtained. The drug business, of which Van Deusen Brothers, Clarke, DuBois, and Kennedy are most prominent, for the sale and manufacture of drugs, oils, etc. Orders are received from several states besides this vicinity.

One felloes for wheels factory, two soap manufactories, one factory for standard scales, pump and block factory. The brick manufacturers are J. H. Cordts & Co., Albert Terry, Nathan Nickerson, P. J. Gurnee, John Streeter & Co., Charles Shultz, Nelson Stephens, A. S. Staples, Jacob Kline. Messrs. Cordts & Co. say they manufacture 135,000 brick daily, amounting for the season, five and one-half months, to 10,500,000. Their estimate for the whole of the brickyards is 75,000,000 of brick. There are five National Banks and three Savings Banks. The Fire Department consists of five steam engines, four hand engines and nine hose companies. The principal hotels are the Eagle Hotel, Kingston Hotel, Mansion House, Hill's Hotel, and there are many others. The ship and boat builders are Allen Brothers, Jefferson McCausland, Lewis Minnerly and Delaware & Hudson Canal Company: one sled manufactory, Crosby, Sahler & Company. There are twenty-two churches in the city, with dates of their organization (a few excepted)—First Reformed Dutch Church, 1659: Fair Street Reformed Dutch Church, 1848: Reformed Dutch Church of the Comforter, 1853: St. John's Episcopal Church, 1832: First Baptist Church, 1832; First Methodist Church, 1824: Second Methodist Church, 1855: Methodist Church, Eddyville, 1835: St. Joseph's Church, Catholic, —— : Presbyterian Church, Rondout, 1833: First Baptist Church, Rondout, 1842; St. Mary's Church, Rondout, 1835; three Jewish churches: St. Peter's German Catholic Church: Methodist Church in Rondout: Church of the Holy Spirit: two Lutheran churches: two Zion (colored) churches.

The Principal of the Kingston Academy is F. J. Cheney, A. M., who has five assistants. The Principals of some of the schools are Professor Henry D. Darrow, William E. Mower, Jared Barhite, John J. Moran, Thomas Raftery, Messrs. Griffin, McCabe and others, each having a large number of assistants. Hon. M. Schoonmaker, Hon. Augustus Schoonmaker, Hon. Frederick L. Westbrook, Postmaster Hayes, E. M. Brigham, Cornelius Burhans, H. D. Baldwin, J. E. Ostrander, Mr. Ridenour and others have by their joint and individual efforts advanced the cause of education until it has attained its present lofty stature and great usefulness to this city. I will simply take some extracts from an able annual report to the Board of Education of 1864, made by Hon. Marius Schoonmaker, for many years President of the Board, relating to the origin, etc., of the Kingston Academy, as follows:

Kingston Academy was originally founded by "the Trustees, Freeholders and commonalty of the town of Kingston," in the year 1774, for the instruction of youth in the learned languages and other branches of knowledge. The names of the Trustees of Kingston for that year, who had the honor of founding this now time honored institution, are Derick Wynkoop, Joseph Gasharie, Johannes Persen, Silvester Salisbury, Christopher Tappen, Adam Persen, Johannes DuBois, Abram Van Gaasbeek, Johannes Sleight, Ezekiel Masten and Wilhelmus Houghtaling. They reserved to themselves the care and superintendence of the institution, and furnished for its use a suitable building and grounds at the corner of Crown and John streets, Kingston. The Academy as thus organized opened and continued a prosperous course under the charge successively of John Addison, Mr. Miller and Mr. Evart, as principals, until the ravages of a desolating war; and the burning of the Academy at the general conflagration at Kingston, 1777, by the British, necessarily suspended instruction for a time. Its trustees soon commenced to repair damages, prepared for its reopening and reconstructed the Academic Hall. The stone building on the southwest corner of John and Crown streets, then occupied as a private residence, was erected and prepared for the accommodation of the Academy, and Mr. Timothy T. Smith was employed as principal December 1, 1792, and notified the public thereof. After its reopening, on the 21st of February, 1794, it again resumed its course of prosperity and celebrity. The trustees of Kingston applied to the Regents of the University of the State of New York for its incorporation. On the 3d of February, 1792, the document was signed by George Clinton as Chancellor. The distinguished character of this institution for many succeeding years and the names of the eminent men of its alumni testify to the wisdom of its policy. Among its alumni are Rev. Dr. Brodhead, Rev. Dr. Thomas DeWitt, Rev. Dr. C. D. Westbrook, and Rev. Dr. Ostrander, who received their preparatory education for college. Its semi-annual examination was looked forward to with great expectations of delight by citizens of Kingston and surrounding country, both old and young, and weeks preceding the event preparations were made for its fitting celebration. At a meeting of the trustees, May 2, 1800, the death of John Addison, the late senior trustee, was announced. The seniority fell upon the Rev. George I. L. Doll. Mr. Smith having resigned his position as principal August 1, 1801. Rev. David Warden was appointed principal tutor. On the 1st day of October, 1802, pursuant to a law passed March 8, 1802, Rev. George I. L. Doll, the then senior trustee, was unanimously elected First President of the Board. Previous to that the senior performed the duties of presiding officer under the title of Mr. Senior. At a meeting of the trustees of the Academy on the 31st day of January, 1804, they resolved to make application to the Regents of the University to found a college. The establishment of a college having been denied, the corporation of Kingston conveyed the whole of the real property which had been designed for a college fund to the trustees of the Kingston Academy, conveying 800 acres of land, including the triangular lot in Kingston upon which in 1834 the present Academy was erected.

The writer of this article will state that on or about 1804, General John Armstrong, known as the boy soldier of the Revolution, Brigadier-General at twenty-five, author of the celebrated Newburgh Letters, and aid to Gen. Gates at the taking of Burgoyne's army, removed to Kingston from Rhinebeck for the better education of his children. To receive the benefits arising from the Kingston Academy under charge of Rev. Mr. Warden (one of those children was afterwards the late Mrs. Wm. B. Astor, of New York), he hired from Mrs. Peter Van Gaasbeck and daughter the old Senate House of 1777, Kingston, she having removed therefrom and resided with her sister, the late Mrs. Rachel Beekman. During its occupancy by General Armstrong, his brother-in-law, Chancellor Livingston, having returned as Minister to the French Court, this eminent man having filled the offices of United States Senator and Secretary of War, was appointed as his successor as Minister to the French Court. General Armstrong engaged Professor

Warden to accompany him to France; he thereupon resigned his office as Principal of Kingston Academy.

At a meeting of the trustees held on the 27th of March, 1830, it was resolved to build a new Academy of brick on the triangular lot. The old Academy building was sold at auction on the 17th of April, 1830. A contract was made to build the Academy in 1834. Mr. Hubbard resigned as principal, and Mr. Isaac A. Blauvelt was appointed to succeed him. On the 31st of December, 1835, Rev. Dr. Gosman, second president, resigned, and Rev. Dr. John Lillie was elected President of the Board.

In 1883 Professor Cheney had been for three years the Principal of the Academy, and his administration has been eminently successful. The enlargement of the Academy edifice has become necessary, and I am gratified to hear that this ancient institution is now again in a flourishing condition, and last evening (June 30th) was held the 109th Annual Commencement in Music Hall, and was witnessed by a very delighted audience.

The writer of this article is not a native of Kingston. About twenty years ago he visited the west, beyond St. Paul, saw many of its prominent cities and places and found that its most prominent were on the west side of the Mississippi. The same thing will be noticed hereafter on our magnificent Hudson. On my return, arriving at Rhinebeck on my way to New York (my place of residence the greater part of my life), my eyes were diverted to the Catskills and its glorious scenery, and observed that in all my travels west there was nothing to compare with the varied and magnificent scenery of Kingston. I had then no pecuniary interest in Kingston whatever. About 1871 I showed Dr. Hoes Miller's History of New York, published in London in 1695 (he subsequently procured a copy). In it were plans of three places, New Amsterdam (now New York), Fort Orange (now Albany), and Kingston, each dated 1695—the only places then of any account in the province of New York. At the time when Congress was selecting the site for the capital of the nation, the several states were called upon to name a suitable place. The State of New York named Kingston; Washington, however, was selected.

In General Sharpe's statement of the old houses now standing at Kingston, the walls of which survived the burning, I think he named forty-six in all. These are our venerable buildings, among which is the Senate House of the State in 1777, where the first Senate was held in the year of the adoption of its first Constitution, of which that great man, Chief Justice Jay, was the author. The walls of this building were erected by Kingston's prominent citizen, Col. Wessel Ten Broeck the elder, about 1676. On the records in the Ulster County Clerk's office, on his being inducted into public office, is his affidavit made about 1676, stating that he was then 40 years old. On the death of the illustrious Thomas Chambers, owner of the Manor of Foxhall, Col. Wessel TenBroeck married his widow. In the annals of Albany it is stated that the TenBroecks' ancestors were descended from the Wessels. He was without doubt the great ancestor of all that bear his honored name.

Citizens of Kingston, preserve these ancient buildings erected on streets laid out by the friend of Kingston, the late Colonial Governor Petrus Stuyvesant, more than 200 years ago, as monuments to remind us of the early sufferings and privations endured by our heroic ancestors from savage and Christian foes. They are, however, slowly disappearing before the changes incident to the onward march of time. Preserve them as relics of a heroic and suffering period, and as vestiges of our country's glory and achievements.

The writer in compiling this article, which he voluntarily assumed, prepared it for publication in one week. Instead of one, four weeks' time should have been allowed to complete what was intended to aid our public spirited men who have completed important public works for the prosperity of Kingston and the welfare of its citizens. I am indebted to Hon. Mr. Lounsbery, Mr. Schepmoes, City Clerk, Gen. Sharpe, Mr. Coykendall, Cornelius Burhans and Mr. Lindsley for valuable information to aid me in this matter.

FREDERICK EDWARD WESTBROOK.

Kingston, June 25, 1883.

COMPLIMENTARY LETTERS.

Among numerous letters received relative to Kingston Senate House, the writer will insert copies of only a few thereof. He was desirous of including a letter received from Martha J. Lamb, the elegant and accomplished historian of the city of New York, which letter being mislaid, in lieu thereof will insert a copy of one received from the former owner and editor of the Kingston *Daily Freeman* and *Weekly Freeman and Journal*, Mr. Charles Marseilles, whose health is substantially restored. Commencing said copies with two received from the late distinguished President Hasbrouck, of Rutgers College, New Jersey : also in their order of dates, one from that eminent historian, Hon. Benson J. Lossing.

KINGSTON, N. Y., April 7, 1875.

Dear Sir :—

I can give you no further information relative to the house you speak of [meaning Senate House], now occupied by my friend, Rev. Dr. Van Santvoord, beyond what is mentioned in your letter of inquiry. The facts as stated by Mrs. TenBroeck are no doubt authentic. As I mentioned to you in our last interview, I remember that Gen. Armstrong occupied the house with his family at the time of his appointment to the French Embassy by President Jefferson.

I sympathize with your efforts to perpetuate the history of this old settlement dating back as long as 1614, when a fort was erected in this vicinity. The traditions of the past are fast fading away. I trust you will succeed in gathering them up.

Respectfully yours,

A. BRUYN HASBROUCK.

FRED'K E. WESTBROOK, Esq., New York City.

KINGSTON, N. Y., May 18, 1875.

My Dear Sir :—

A score of the little hindrances that are apt to occur even in the leisurely path of an aged man have prevented me from making an earlier acknowledgement of your kind letter. I needed not this demonstration of your love of antiquarian research in a county in which you are by descent so closely associated.

Our Ulster Historical Society commenced well. The war called away most of our active members, and its meetings were suspended during its progress. I made one or two unsuccessful efforts afterwards to revive it and resign my presidency for a more efficient superintendence, but nothing has of late been done and the society now, if not dead, is at least in a very sound sleep. A rich mine is still to be worked which the society only opened.

I regret to say our collections are out of print and I fear I shall not be able to supply your wants. I have from time to time applications made to me, even from distant States, for copies of our collections, which I regret I cannot furnish. You are fortunate in procuring the two numbers you mention. Among other papers which would interest you are papers on the settlement of New Paltz, by Edmund Elting; a history of the church there from its first establishment by the Huguenots, by Dr. Stitt, and a very full history of Vaughan's expedition up the Hudson and the burning of Kingston, &c., by Col. Pratt, whose death was a severe loss to the society.

If any of these, or others which you have not, should unexpectedly fall in my way you shall have them.

Believe me, resp'y yours,
A. BRUYN HASBROUCK.

FRED'K E. WESTBROOK, Esq., New York.

THE RIDGE, DOVER PLAINS, May 28, 1883.

My Dear Sir :—

Please accept my cordial thanks for your kind courtesy in sending me an impression of an engraving of your summer residence at Kingston, the old Senate House of 1777, and hallowed by the lapse of years since it was built and by the precious historical associations which cluster around it.

In 1848, while at Kingston, I made a sketch of a stone house on the south-west corner of Maiden Lane and Fair street, then the residence of Mr. Baldwin (since torn down). I was then informed that the house named was the one in which the State Convention was held when that body adopted the State Constitution.

I hope to have the pleasure of meeting you at Fishkill next Saturday on the occasion of a Centennial celebration, where I expect to have the pleasure and profit of listening to a historical oration from the lips of your brother, Judge T. R. Westbrook.

Yours, very truly,
BENSON J. LOSSING.

FREDERICK E. WESTBROOK, Esq.

EXETER, NEW HAMPSHIRE, August 27, 1883.

FRED. E. WESTBROOK, Esq. :

My Dear Sir :—I see by the Freeman, which I receive daily, that you are still in Kingston, and that you had the old Senate House gorgeously decorated on the occasion of the recent Firemen's Convention in that city. * * * * If the State had more public-spirited citizens like you the old Senate House would not remain long the property of a private citizen, but would become the property of the State. The State ought, certainly, to be in the possession for all time of that building, which fills so important a place in the history of New York.

I understand that the population of Kingston is rapidly increasing. By the way, perhaps you are aware that Exeter, here in New Hampshire, was the original capital of the State as Kingston was of New York.

Sincerely yours,

CHARLES MARSEILLES.

NEWBURGH, N. Y., Sept. 5th, 1883.

FRED. E. WESTBROOK, Esq :

My Dear Sir :—Please accept my thanks for your reminiscences of the early history of the city of Kingston, and especially the photograph of the Wessel Ten Broeck mansion, since occupied as the Senate building of 1777. Although personally unacquainted with you, I knew your father, Rev. Dr. Westbrook, quite well, and recollect distinctly his accepting the editorial department of the *Christian Intelligencer*, at its inception, and which I have continued to read from that day. It was my pleasure to spend a week in Kingston during the session of General Synod, some years since, where I enjoyed the hospitality of your brother, Judge Westbrook, with whom and his family I formed a very pleasant acquaintance ; to whom please extend my regards.

Hoping we may in the near future become more intimately acquainted, I am

Sincerely and truly yours,

THOMAS JESSUP.

FISHKILL-ON-THE-HUDSON, Sept. 18, 1883.

My dear Mr. Westbrook :—

I acknowledge with pleasure your interesting and welcome letter, and warmly congratulate you on the success which your historical writings are receiving. I shall be very happy to see your pamphlet. I suppose you have seen in the last *Harper's Weekly*, Sept. 15th, a picture of your historic Senate House, in the interesting article on the old capital at Albany, recently taken down.

I am, as you know, very fond of such historical studies, and they open to me fields of rare delight.

I thank you for your kind mention of my Fishkill centennial address.

Your brother gave an eloquent address, and Judge Graham, of Newburgh, acquitted himself well.

Very truly, with kind remembrance to the Judge,

J. HERVEY COOK.

CLOSING REMARKS.

． ·

THE FISHKILL CENTENNIAL.

June 2, 1883, was a grand day for glorious old Fishkill, Dutchess County, N. Y., (writer's native town). Five thousand persons participated in the Fishkill Centennial of the disbandment of a detachment of Washington's army at Fishkill village during its five years' service in the war of the Revolution. The house which Washington occupied while at Fishkill, still standing, was the residence of Colonel John Brinckerhoof, a man of distinguished reputation, and with whom Washington advised and frequently spent days at his home.

At 2.30 P. M., a Revolutionary cannon was fired thirteen times in honor of the then thirteen States, and the procession moved, headed by Piano's band ; next was Dr. C. Kittridge's choir of male singers, next the Fishkill centennial committee, the clergy, the speakers and the thirty-eight young ladies representing the thirty-eight states.

Hon. Benson J. Lossing was chairman, assisted by thirteen vice-presidents. Among these were Mr. Brett, over ninety years of age, and General Schofield, an officer in the army of 1812.

The proceedings commenced with prayer by Rev. Robert Van Kleeck, followed by Judge Monell, of Fishkill, chairman of the committee of arrangements, who delivered an able address. When alluding to the thirty-eight young ladies on the platform, the judge said blushingly : "The representatives of the stars, and the blue ground of the flag ; also, Heaven's first best gift to man. Let the toast be, 'Dear woman,' and let the band respond." This seemed to largely increase the fervor and the patriotism of the occasion.

Mr. Lossing then introduced Hon. T. R. Westbrook, of Kingston, who delivered the first historical address. Then followed J. Hervey Cook, Esq., the historian of Fishkill, who delivered an able address. Judge Graham, of Newburgh, was the next speaker. He was listened to with marked attention. Mr. Lossing then announced that a poem by Mary Westbrook would be published with the proceedings.

Music, prayer, and the benediction by Rev. Mr. Thomas, pastor of the Revolutionary Dutch church of the village, closed the proceedings, which will long be remembered by all present.

．

THE NEWBURGH CENTENNIAL.

October 18, 1883, at Washington's headquarters, city of Newburgh, will be celebrated with great pomp and splendor the one hundredth anniversary of its occupation by the illustrious Washington, at the closing scenes of the successful war for liberty and independence, on that august and memorable occasion in the presence of the President of the United States and representatives from many of its states and others who will on that occasion assemble to witness the laying of the corner stone of the monument for which Congress has appropriated $35,000, to hear the statesman and orator, Mr. Evarts; to see the grand parade and ships of the American navy riding at anchor gracing the silvery waters of the majestic Hudson; the grand old Fishkill mountains with their rich and fertile valleys (the native town of the writer), all conspiring to cause the bay of Newburgh always to be the most commanding and most beautiful view that presents itself to the beholder anywhere on the waters of the noble Hudson, which on this occasion will present an animated and never to be forgotten scene.

Newburgh has its honored Headquarters; Kingston possesses the old Senate House of 1777, whose walls survive the lapse of time and the power and efforts of the enemy, and will continue for centuries to come. Guard and protect these venerable relics of a suffering period, as monuments to perpetuate the remembrance of the actors of those mighty scenes, long sleeping in death, and of our country's glory, and to serve as a fraternal bond of union that ought always to exist between the cities of Newburgh and Kingston, who were at an early period sharers in common sufferings, as they are now enjoying the blessing of lasting peace.

General Arthur, President of the United States, who is to be present, has visited Kingston's Senate House on a former occasion.

Let there be a general movement of the patriots of Kingston for Newburgh on the 18th of October (within one hour's ride) to witness this grand uprising of the people on that memorable day.

FREDERICK EDWARD WESTBROOK.

Kingston, October 16, 1883.

www.ingramcontent.com/pod-product-compliance
Lightning Source LLC
Chambersburg PA
CBHW021428090426
42739CB00009B/1397